The Dumpling Cookbook

The Dumpling Cookbook

By Maria Polushkin

Workman Publishing Company, New York

Library of Congress Cataloging in Publication Data

Polushkin, Maria
  The dumpling cookbook.
  Includes index.

  1. Dumplings.   I. Title.
TX770.P63   641.6'3'1   76-25437
ISBN 0-911104-81-X
ISBN 0-911104-85-2 pbk.

Jacket and book design: Paul Hanson
Jacket photograph: Cosimo
Illustrations: Pat Stewart

Workman books are available at special discounts
when purchased in bulk for premiums and sales pro-
motions as well as for fund-raising or educational
use. Special editions or book excerpts can also
be created to specification. For details, contact the
Special Sales Director at the address below.

Workman Publishing Company
708 Broadway
New York, N.Y. 10003

Manufactured in the United States of America
First printing January 1977
15   14   13   12   11

To my mother,
whose delicious vareniki, piroshki,
and chebureki inspired a lifelong
love of dumplings

and to my father,
whose robust appetite inspired me
to learn to make them.

Contents

The Dropped Dumplings

The Filled Dumplings

The Fritters

The Sweet Dumplings

The Sauces

Introduction

With the exception of bread, no other prepared food I can think of has the universality of the dumpling. The very word is a joy and conjures up indefinite images suffused with feelings of affection and love of food.

Why indefinite? Because no one seems to be very sure just what is and what is not a dumpling. After a year of research and a lifetime of enthusiastic eating, I'm still not sure myself. *Webster's International Dictionary* supplies the following definition: "Dumpling (diminutive of 'dump', an ill-shaped piece). A small light mass of baking powder biscuit dough cooked either by boiling, as with soup or stew with which it is to be served, or by steaming or baking, especially when it contains fruit such as apples or cherries."

But the lexicographers were wrong. For one thing, while most dumplings do have some sort of dough in them, it varies considerably. In some cases it's just flour or bread mixed with a liquid, and at other times a yeast dough is called for. Often the dough is stuffed with something. The shape is as important as the method of cooking. It is my opinion, and the guiding principle of this book, that a dumpling must be "immersed" or "dumped" into a cooking medium—be it water, soup, hot fat, or even steam.

Like many things that are both simple and elegant in our Western heritage, dumplings come originally from the East. Every school child knows that spaghetti came to Italy from Cathay, via Marco Polo, but fewer people realize that ravioli (that archetypical stuffed dumpling), and indeed every basic kind of dumpling, also came from China. And today there is hardly a part of the world that doesn't have dumplings in the national cuisine. Unfortunately, most historians have been remarkably reticent about the dumpling diaspora. Pliny the Elder has little to say; Gibbon is silent altogether.

In the absence of historical record I can only guess that before Marco Polo brought his prizes to Italy, the Mongols and other nomads took the dumpling from China to Siberia and thence to Russia. Russian pelmeni, Mongolian manty, and the basic Chinese stuffed dumplings are all remarkably similar. Perhaps the Jews took the idea of pelmeni and made kreplach; I don't really know, of course, but I do know that nearly every nation has its variations on the dumpling theme. Austria has specknödle, Germany has Konigsberger klops, Mexico has albondigas, Korea has mandoo, Italy has gnocchi, France has quenelles, Manhattan has matzoh balls. It goes on and on.

Wherever they come from and wherever they are found, dumplings are basically a peasant food. Poor people have always been the most ingenious cooks because they have always had to make do with the meagerest fare. They have had to find ways to make a small bit of meat stretch to feed a large number of people. Or they have had to find ways to make a pot of soup filling enough to be an entire meal. The dumpling, in one guise or another, fills the bill. It is a meat stretcher par excellence, and in its heavenly starchy incarnation it turns a pot of stew or soup into a gut-filling, soul-satisfying experience.

As I've indicated, the word "dumpling" denotes the widest possible variety of prepared foods, and before any more can be said, it is perhaps necessary to mention that for the purposes of organizing this book I have divided dumplings into three main categories: dropped dumplings, filled dumplings, and fritters.

"Dropped dumpling" is my word for those dumplings of more or less homogeneous texture which are made by dropping a prepared mixture into boiling water, soup, or stew. All dropped dumplings contain starch in one form or another. Indeed, many people know dumplings primarily as an interesting substitute for the more common starch dishes such as potatoes, rice, or bread. The degree to which other ingredients enter into the mixture, or even dominate it, will often determine whether the dish can ultimately stand on its own as a course.

The simplest kind of dropped dumplings, for instance the plain butter dumpling, consists primarily of flour, eggs, and butter. Yet these simple ingredients, when mixed together and dropped into a boiling soup, instantly turn that unassuming soup into something you can really eat. The starchier dumplings are essentially foils for, and enhancers of, the flavors of the basic foods which they accompany. That is the quintessential idea of the dumpling. (Stews, ragouts, and fricassees are all, of course, very like soup, only thicker, and with more emphasis on meats. Some people, including myself, only consider a good stew worth eating if there is a delicious starchy morsel at hand to mop up the gravy. Dumplings are made with this in mind.)

To the basic dropped dumpling recipes have come the inevitable refinements. Other ingredients are added to the dough mixture—herbs, spices, cheese, vegetables, and bits of meat. As these savory ingredients dominate the basic starch mixture, the role that the dish can play in a meal begins to expand. Ham dumplings or malfatti (Italian spinach and cheese dumplings) stand on their own quite well as a light course. Konigsberger klops have even less starch and make a wonderful main course. There is no dogma when it comes to dumplings. Forcemeat dumplings can be served in soup while well-sauced starchy dumplings can be a meal by themselves.

If the versatility of dropped dumplings is impressive, that of filled dumplings is nothing less than spectacular. With the starchy element (in this case, dough) forming a kind of protective shell on the outside, they tend to blend less with surrounding foods, and thereby make any meal a more varied taste experience.

There is something universally appealing about filled dumplings— perhaps the element of surprise, or the contrasting textures of filling and shell, or even some secret pride or pleasure in the slightly greater amount of work involved. Whatever the reason, they are unfailingly popular. If you have ever served them to hungry guests, you know that you can never make enough of them.

Dropped dumplings, as we have seen, are invariably boiled. Filled dumplings, however, can be boiled, steamed, fried, or even baked. Indeed, almost any basic recipe for filled dumplings can yield surprisingly different results if different methods of cooking are used. Most people, for instance, have eaten wontons as boiled dumplings in a bowl of Chinese soup, though the very same dumplings, fried in hot oil and served with sweet and sour sauce, can be a gustatory experience of another order.

Like a good actor, a filled dumpling can play almost any role. Wontons, pelmeni, and kreplach are all traditionally served in a simple broth, yet each can also be served alone with butter, cheese, sour cream, or other garnish. Ravioli is traditionally served with a sauce, but there is no reason not to simply drop them in a pot of broth.

I have included a third category, fritters, in this book because of certain obvious connections they have to both dropped and filled dumplings. Characteristically, they are deep fried in hot fat and the starchy element is invariably a kind of batter. As with dropped dumplings, the ingredients may be mixed thoroughly with the batter and dropped into the cooking medium. A good example is corn fritters. Or, as with filled dumplings, the batter may be used to form a crisp outer coating. The most elaborate example of this is tempura.

Fritters are simple to prepare and lend themselves to the widest possible range of ingredients. They are a particularly nice way of preparing fresh fruit and vegetables, since the high heat and short cooking time preserve delicate flavor and freshness. I need make no special introduction to sweet dumplings. Each of the three categories of dumplings includes a healthy sampling of these. Although an obvious choice for dessert, many sweet dumplings such as calas or fruit-filled vareniki are more appropriate for breakfast, snacks, or lunch.

I hope I've whetted your appetite and convinced you of the infinite variety and downright goodness of dumplings. But if these remarks have not done the job, I refer you directly to the recipes;

they are far more eloquent than I.

If there is one last word to say on the subject, it is that the history of dumplings is, more than anything, a history of experimentation. The recipes in this book are just a beginning. Many I simply improvised; some were devised by friends or acquaintances; still more are traditional, which is to say only that they were made up a long time ago. After all these years, the possibilities are still unlimited. If you would like a wider sampling of recipes, I refer you to your own imagination.

The Dropped Dumplings

Notes on dropped dumplings

Unlike the filled dumpling, which has a shell of dough, the dropped dumpling is a homogeneous mixture of ingredients. I have called these the "dropped dumplings" because they are cooked by being "dropped" into simmering or boiling liquid. Once in the liquid, the dumplings drop to the bottom of the pot like stones, but in a few minutes come floating up to the surface, puffed up, delicate, and light.

It is the dropped dumplings that most people think of when they think "dumpling." Dropped dumplings float in a soup, liven up a stew, complement a roast. Like all dumplings, they can turn an ordinary dish into a special one. Of course, they are terrific emergency meal extenders and meat stretchers. But contrary to common opinion, dropped dumplings do not always appear in a supporting role. There are dumplings that insist on being served as a course by themselves, such as the various Italian gnocchi. And there are meat dumplings, poached and sauced and astonishingly succulent, that provide

Drop dumplings into boiling broth.

unusual and delicious main courses.

The dumplings in this section range from the simplest, such as the butter dumplings for soup (made literally in minutes), to the most subtle and sublime of poached dumplings, the fish quenelles. Most of these are very simple to make. Aside from the ingredients called for in the recipes you will need a pot large enough to hold 6 to 8 quarts of water, a large slotted spoon or skimmer to remove the dumplings from the simmering liquid, and a strainer.

Butter Dumplings for soup

These lovely golden dumplings are an enrichment to almost any soup. They are especially good with a fresh pea soup.* Best of all, you can make them in minutes.

2 *eggs*
½ *cup all-purpose flour*
6 *tablespoons (¾ stick) butter, softened to room temperature*
½ *teaspoon salt*
¼ *teaspoon nutmeg*
1½–2 *quarts beef or chicken broth, or other soup*

1. In a medium bowl, beat the eggs. Add the flour and mix.

2. Into the flour mixture beat the butter, salt, and nutmeg to make a smooth batter.

3. Bring the soup to a boil. Drop half-teaspoonfuls of the batter into the gently boiling soup. Cook 6 to 7 minutes. Serve dumplings in the soup.

Serves 6 to 8.

Notes and Variations

*Fresh pea soup is easy to make. To 1½ quarts of boiling water, add about 3 pounds of peas in their pods, 1 small grated onion, and an assortment of herbs, such as parsley, tarragon and marjoram. Simmer, uncovered, for ½ hour. Press everything through the coarsest blade of a food mill, and then again through the finest blade. Return to the saucepan, season with salt and pepper and a little fresh mint, if you like. Bring the soup to a boil, drop in the dumplings, and cook until they are done. For extra richness, add 3 to 4 tablespoons of heavy cream just before serving.

Parsley Dumplings for stew

This is it—the all-purpose, all-American, delicious dumpling for stews, soups, chowders, ragouts, or fricassees.

2 cups all-purpose flour
3 teaspoons baking powder
1 teaspoon salt
½ teaspoon sugar
⅓ cup finely chopped parsley
¼ teaspoon thyme
¼ teaspoon nutmeg
¼ teaspoon ground cloves
　Several grindings black pepper
2 tablespoons butter
¾ cup boiling water
　Approximately 2 quarts stew or soup

1. Sift together the flour, baking powder, salt, and sugar into a large bowl. Add the parsley, thyme, nutmeg, cloves, and pepper. Mix well.

2. Cut in the butter and add enough of the boiling water to make a stiff batter.

3. Bring the stew or soup to a boil. Drop tablespoonfuls of the batter into the boiling stew or soup. Simmer for 10 minutes uncovered, then cover and cook 5 minutes more.

Yield: About 16 to 20 dumplings; serves 6 to 8.

Notes and Variations

These dumplings can be varied with an infinite number of herbs and seasonings. Try some of the following combinations, or invent your own.

1. Omit the nutmeg and cloves, and add ½ teaspoon of sage and 2 tablespoons of grated onion.

2. Omit parsley, thyme, nutmeg, and cloves, and add 3 teaspoons of caraway seeds.

3. Add 2 to 3 tablespoons of grated sharp cheese.

4. Substitute any other fresh herbs, such as tarragon, for the parsley.

Matzoh Balls

No matter how many aunts, mothers, and grandmothers you have heard of who make the "best" matzoh balls, forget it! *These* are the best. Serve them in chicken broth, of course, but matzoh balls are wonderful in chicken or any other kind of stew.

½ stick butter, or ¼ cup rendered chicken fat, softened to room temperature
2 eggs
½ teaspoon salt
2 tablespoons finely chopped parsley
  Several grindings black pepper
½ cup matzoh meal
  Approximately 1½ quarts chicken broth

1. In a medium bowl, blend the butter or chicken fat with the eggs, salt, parsley, and pepper.

2. Stir in the matzoh meal. Cover and refrigerate for 1 hour.

3. With wet hands, form the dough into walnut-size balls. Set them on a cookie sheet, cover, and refrigerate for at least ½ hour.

4. Bring the chicken broth to a boil. Drop the matzoh balls into the boiling broth. Cover and simmer for 15 minutes. Test a matzoh ball to see if it is fluffy throughout. If so, they are done. Serve them in the chicken broth.

Yield: About 18 matzoh balls; serves 4 to 6.

Liver Dumplings for soup

2 tablespoons butter
1 small onion, coarsely sliced
¼ pound liver, any kind, cut into ½-inch
    pieces
1 egg
2 tablespoons finely chopped parsley
¼ teaspoon thyme
½ teaspoon salt
    Several grindings black pepper
1½ slices of stale bread, sprinkled with 5
    tablespoons of milk
¼ cup all-purpose flour
    Approximately 2 quarts beef or chicken
    broth

1. In a medium skillet, melt the butter and sauté the sliced onion until it is soft.

2. Add the liver pieces and brown quickly on all sides. Remove from heat.

3. Chop the liver and onion together, or put through a meat grinder.

4. Beat the egg until frothy and add it to the liver mixture, along with the parsley, thyme, salt, and pepper. Mix well.

5. Squeeze excess milk from the bread and crumble it into the liver mixture. Mix and add just enough of the flour to make a soft dough.

6. Bring the broth to a boil. Drop teaspoonfuls of the dough into the boiling broth and simmer 3 to 4 minutes. Serve the dumplings in the soup.

Serves 6 to 8.

Mashed Potato Dumplings

Using leftovers creatively can be an art. My friend, Ronnie Shushan, specializes in turning hopeless-looking leftovers into appetizing dishes. Since nothing looks less inspiring than cold mashed potatoes, and since the dumplings that are made from them are among my favorites, I dedicate this recipe to her. Never throw out leftover mashed potatoes—use them for these quick, easy and delicious dumplings.

1 *cup cold mashed potatoes*
½ *cup all-purpose flour*
1 *egg*
  Salt and pepper to taste
  Approximately 2 quarts stew or soup

1. In a medium bowl, mix together the first 4 ingredients to form a stiff dough.

2. Roll the dough out and cut it into 2-inch square dumplings.

3. Bring the stew or soup to a boil. Drop the dumplings into the boiling stew or soup. Cover and simmer for 10 minutes.

Serves 4 to 6.

Eastern European Vegetable Dumplings

These dumplings are terrific with boiled beef and roasts. For added interest serve with a bowl of sour cream.

1 *stick butter*
1 *celery knob, finely chopped*
1 *carrot, finely chopped*
1 *medium onion, finely chopped*
½ *head of cauliflower, finely chopped*
4 *hard rolls, diced and soaked in ⅔ cup milk*
2 *eggs*
4 *tablespoons all-purpose flour*
1 *teaspoon salt*
  Several grindings black pepper
7–8 *quarts of salted water*

1. In a large skillet, melt half the butter. Sauté the celery, carrot, and onion for 15 minutes. Stir occasionally.

2. Add the cauliflower, and continue cooking another 15 minutes.

3. Squeeze excess milk from the rolls and crumble them into a bowl. Add the eggs and mix. Stir in flour, then add the cooked vegetables, salt, and pepper. Mix well.

4. Form walnut-size dumplings.

5. Bring the salted water to a boil. Drop the dumplings into the boiling water. Simmer for 12 to 15 minutes. Test to see if done. Drain.

6. Melt the remaining butter and brown the dumplings in butter for about 5 minutes.

Serves 8.

Csipetke tiny Hungarian dumplings

In Hungary, csipetke are served with goulash—which makes them the perfect accompaniment for any stew. Csipetke are a great deal of fun to make with children because rolling the tiny little balls seems to be perfectly suited for small hands. Fun to make, fun to eat—what more could be asked of a dumpling?

3½ *cups all-purpose flour*
 1 *teaspoon salt*
 2 *eggs*
   Approximately ⅓ cup water

1. Mix the flour, salt, and eggs together and add just enough water to form a stiff dough. Knead the dough for about 5 minutes.

2. Roll the dough out to a thickness of about ½ inch and then cut it into ½-inch wide strips.

3. Pinch off small pieces, each about the size of a bean, and shape the pieces into tiny balls.

4. Cook the csipetke in a large pot of boiling water for about 5 minutes until they float to the top or drop them directly into bubbling stew.

Serves 4 to 6.

Spaetzle   tiny German dumplings

Spaetzle, "little sparrows," are very like hornli, "little horns," and knopfli, "little buttons." They are all tiny dumplings, very popular in Germany and Switzerland. A plateful of these lovely golden nuggets can be a meal in itself, with salad and wine. Otherwise, serve them with chicken, game, or meat. The purchase of a spaetzle mill will simplify the procedure of making them, although you can certainly make do with a large-hole colander, or even a wooden board and a sharp knife.

3 *cups all-purpose flour*
4 *eggs*
1 *teaspoon salt*
  Several grindings black pepper
1 *cup warm water*
  Approximately 4 quarts of salted water
½ *stick butter*

1. In a large bowl, combine the flour with the eggs, salt, pepper, and warm water. Beat hard with a wooden spoon to form a thick, smooth batter. Continue beating for 5 minutes. This should be done rather energetically, by scraping the dough toward you with a regular rhythm, so as to incorporate as much air as possible.

2. Let the dough rest, covered, for 15 minutes, then beat it for another 5 minutes.

3. Bring the salted water to a boil.

4. If you are using a spaetzle mill, simply push the dough through it into the boiling salted water. If you do not have a

A spaetzle mill.

Press dough through the holes of a colander with a large wooden spoon.

mill, balance a colander (the largest you own) on the rim of the pot in which the water is boiling. Make sure that the water is at least 8 inches below the colander or the dough will simply congeal from the steam. Use a large wooden spoon to press the dough through the holes in the colander into the water. A third alternative is to add a little more flour to the dough (about ½ cup) to stiffen it. Remove the dough to a floured board and with a sharp knife slice it into strips about ¼ inch wide and ½ inch long.

5. Boil the spaetzle for 4 minutes. Drain in a large colander, and rinse briefly under cold running water. Drain.*

6. Melt the butter in an ovenproof skillet. Sauté the spaetzle for 3 to 4 minutes, then place the skillet in a 350° oven and bake for 10 minutes.

Serves 6 to 8.

Notes and Variations

*You can make the spaetzle ahead up to this point. Spread them out on a kitchen towel and cover them with a damp towel. They will keep for several hours.

Specknödel
Austrian bacon dumplings

Knödel and klösse are German words for dumplings. There seems to be an infinite variety of knödel and klösse in Germany, Austria, and other European dumpling-eating countries. Specknödel are dumplings with the addition of bacon. Served in broth, they turn a bowl of soup into a hearty meal. Or cook them in boiling salted water and serve them on a bed of steaming sauerkraut with boiled sausage.

¼ *pound slab bacon, diced into small pieces*
2 *cups stale bread, cut into ½-inch cubes*
1 *medium onion, finely chopped*
¼ *cup milk*
½ *cup flour*
½ *cup finely chopped parsley*
1 *tablespoon caraway seeds*
Several grindings black pepper
Approximately 3 quarts salted water

1. In a large skillet, fry the diced bacon until the pieces are crisp. Remove the bacon and drain on absorbent paper. Remove 2 tablespoons of the rendered bacon fat and reserve.

2. Add the bread cubes to the fat remaining in the skillet and fry them until they are well-toasted. Remove the bread cubes to a bowl.

3. Add the 2 tablespoons of reserved bacon fat to the skillet and sauté the onion until it is just golden.

4. Add the bacon and onion to the bread cubes along with the milk, flour, parsley, caraway seeds, and pepper. Knead with your hands to make a dough. Shape into walnut-size balls.

5. Bring the salted water to a boil. Drop the balls into the boiling water and simmer for 10 to 12 minutes. Remove with slotted spoon, drain, and serve.

Serves 4 to 6.

Notes and Variations

If you are going to serve specknödel in soup, you can cook them directly in the broth.

Bread Dumplings

Never throw out stale bread, there are hundreds of good uses for it. One of the best is making these toothsome dumplings. Of all the dumplings I've tried, I like these the best for sopping up gravy.

½ *stick butter*
1 *medium onion, finely chopped*
3 *cups stale bread, cut into ½-inch cubes*
¼ *cup all-purpose flour, plus additional flour*
      for shaping dumplings
¼ *teaspoon baking powder*
1 *egg, lightly beaten*
½ *cup finely chopped parsley*
1 *tablespoon caraway seeds*
1 *teaspoon salt*
   Several grindings black pepper
¼ *cup milk*
   Approximately 2 quarts soup or stew

1. In a skillet, melt the butter, and sauté the onion until it is light brown. Add the bread cubes and cook, stirring, until they are toasted.

2. Remove the onion and bread cubes to a bowl. Add the flour, baking powder, egg, parsley, caraway seeds, salt, and pepper. Mix well and add the milk.

3. Knead the mixture with your hands to form a dough. Let stand for 15 minutes. Shape the dough into walnut-size balls. Roll each ball in flour.

4. Bring the soup or stew to a boil. Drop the dumplings into the boiling soup or stew and simmer, uncovered, for 5 minutes. Cover, and simmer 3 minutes longer.

Serves 4 to 6.

Notes and Variations

1. An alternative is to shape the dough into 2 loaves and tie them in cheese cloth which has been dredged in flour. This helps to keep the shape. Refrigerate them for 1 hour, then lower the loaves into 2 quarts of simmering salted water and cook for 25 minutes. Drain, remove the cheese cloth, and serve in slices.

2. To vary the flavor, substitute ¼ cup of bacon fat or rendered chicken fat for the ½ stick butter.

Bread and Potato Dumplings

Make these dumplings when you are feeling poor and hungry. They will fill you up and make you feel better. Try them with applesauce. They are also good with chicken and meat.

6 *medium potatoes*
10 *slices of bread soaked in water*
1 *large onion, finely chopped or grated*
2 *eggs, well beaten*
2 *tablespoons finely chopped parsley*
1 *teaspoon salt*
  Several grindings black pepper
  Flour to roll dumplings in
6–8 *quarts salted water*

To serve
1 *cup breadcrumbs sautéed in ½ stick butter*

1. Peel the potatoes and grate them. Place them in a kitchen towel and squeeze out as much moisture as possible. Put them in a medium bowl.

2. Squeeze excess water from the bread and crumble it onto the grated potatoes.

3. Add the onion, eggs, parsley, salt, and pepper to the potato mixture. Stir to mix well.

4. Form the mixture into walnut-size balls and roll them in flour.

5. Bring the salted water to a boil. Drop dumplings into the boiling water, 8 to 10 at a time. Cook for 15 to 20 minutes.

6. Remove the cooked dumplings with a slotted spoon to a buttered ovenproof dish. Keep them warm in a slow (250°) oven until all are done.

7. Top with the sautéed breadcrumbs and serve.

Serves 6 to 8.

Kluski Polish dumplings

Although these dumplings are good served with a pot roast or stewed chicken, I like them for breakfast. Decide for yourself.

2 *cups well-drained, large-curd cottage cheese, farmer cheese, or pot cheese*
1 *tablespoon butter, softened to room temperature*
1 *teaspoon salt*
3 *eggs, separated, plus* 1 *egg yolk*
1 *cup all-purpose flour*
  Approximately 2 *quarts salted water*

To serve
1 *cup breadcrumbs sautéed in* ½ *stick butter*

1. Press the cheese through a sieve into a bowl. Blend in the softened butter. Add the salt, egg yolks, and flour. Blend well.

2. Beat the egg whites until they are stiff and fold them into the cheese mixture.

3. Bring the salted water to a boil. Drop tablespoonfuls of the batter into the boiling water. Cook about 5 minutes, or until they float to the top. Test one to see if it is cooked all the way through before removing all the kluski with a slotted spoon.

4. Cover the hot kluski with the sautéed breadcrumbs and serve.

Serves 4 to 6.

Notes and Variations

If you are not going to serve the kluski immediately, arrange them in a buttered baking dish and keep warm in a slow (250°) oven.

Tomatoes and Dumplings

Fluffy dumplings, cooked with seasoned tomatoes, make a delicious, old-fashioned side dish to serve with meat.

Tomatoes

½ stick butter
1 medium onion, finely chopped
1 carrot, finely chopped
1 stick celery, finely chopped
4 cups canned whole tomatoes
2 teaspoons sugar
1 teaspoon crushed fennel seed
1 teaspoon salt
   Several grindings black pepper

Dumplings

1 cup all-purpose flour
2 teaspoons baking powder
½ teaspoon salt
1 tablespoon butter
½ cup milk

1. In a heavy saucepan, melt the butter. Add the onion, carrot, and celery and sauté for 5 minutes.

2. Add the tomatoes, sugar, and seasonings. Bring to a boil and simmer while you make the dumpling dough.

3. Into a medium bowl, sift together the flour, baking powder, and salt. Blend in the butter with a pastry cutter or two knives until the flour mixture resembles coarse oatmeal.

4. Add the milk and stir to form a soft dough. Cover and let stand for 10 to 15 minutes.

5. Drop tablespoonfuls of the dough into the simmering tomatoes. Cover and cook for 10 to 15 minutes.

Serves 6 to 8.

Halushky

In the Ukraine they are called halushky; in neighboring Czechoslovakia they are knedliki. They should be extremely light and tender. Serve these dumplings, smothered with fried onions, instead of other starches. I like them with a salad for lunch.

¾ cup all-purpose flour
¾ cup uncooked farina
2 teaspoons baking powder
1 teaspoon salt
½ stick cold butter
2 eggs, lightly beaten
¼ cup milk or buttermilk
  Approximately 6 to 8 quarts salted water

Topping

2 large onions, thinly sliced
½ stick butter
  Sour cream (optional)

1. In a large bowl, combine the flour, farina, baking powder, and salt. Mix well.

2. Add the butter in small pieces. Crumble the flour mixture with your fingertips to form a coarse meal.

3. Add the eggs and milk. Stir until the batter is smooth.

4. Bring the salted water to a boil. Using two tablespoons, drop the batter into the boiling water. Cover, and simmer for 8 minutes. Cook 6 to 8 at a time.

5. Remove cooked dumplings from the water with a slotted spoon and place them in a buttered ovenproof dish. Keep warm in a slow (250°) oven until all the dumplings and the topping are done.

6. To prepare the topping, melt the butter in a skillet. Sauté the sliced onions until they are light brown and starting to crisp. Remove from heat.

7. Cover the dumplings with the fried onions. Serve accompanied by a bowl of sour cream, if you wish.

Yield: About 12 to 15 dumplings.

Notes and Variations

Leftover halushky are delicious fried in butter or bacon fat.

Ham Dumplings

A great way to use stale bread. Ham dumplings and a good green salad make a delicious and inexpensive meal.

¾ cup milk
3 cups stale bread, cut into ½-inch cubes
1 stick butter
½ pound cooked ham, finely ground
3 eggs
½ cup finely chopped parsley
½ cup dry cottage or farmer cheese
½ teaspoon salt
  Several grindings black pepper
  Flour to roll dumplings in
  Approximately 2 quarts salted water

Topping

½ stick butter
1 medium onion, finely chopped
¼ pound mushrooms, finely chopped
½ cup breadcrumbs
½ cup finely chopped parsley
  Salt and pepper to taste

1. Pour the milk over the bread cubes and let stand about 20 minutes.

2. In a large skillet, melt the butter and sauté the bread cubes until they turn a nice brown color. Remove them to a bowl. Add the ham, eggs, parsley, cottage or farmer cheese, salt, and pepper to the bread cubes. Mix well.

3. Shape the mixture into walnut-size balls and roll in flour.

4. Bring the salted water to a boil. Drop 6 to 8 dumplings into the boiling water and cook 10 to 12 minutes, or until they rise to the surface.

5. Remove the dumplings with a slotted spoon and arrange in a buttered ovenproof dish. Keep the dumplings warm in a slow (250°) oven while you cook the remaining dumplings and then make the topping.

6. In a skillet, melt the butter for the topping. Sauté the onion and mushrooms until the onion turns light brown in color. Add the breadcrumbs and stir until they are lightly toasted, then mix in the parsley. Add salt and pepper to taste (I like a great deal of black pepper with this). Pour the mixture over the dumplings.

Serves 4 to 6.

Keftedes Greek meat dumplings

These meatball dumplings are very good served with new potatoes, a green salad, and a bottle of earthy Greek wine.

1½ *pounds lean lamb, ground*
2 *slices white bread or 1 hard roll, soaked in water*
1 *medium onion, finely chopped*
1 *garlic clove, finely chopped or put through garlic press*
1 *teaspoon salt*
  Several grindings black pepper
1 *teaspoon oregano*
6–8 *quarts salted water*
  Avgolemono Sauce, page 184

1. Place the ground lamb into a mixing bowl, blender, or bowl of food processor.

2. Squeeze excess water from the bread or roll. Crumble it onto the lamb, along with the onion, garlic, and seasonings.

3. Blend at high speed for several minutes, or knead vigorously with your hands until very smooth.

4. With wet hands, form walnut-size balls. (You can freeze the dumplings at this point for future use.)

5. Bring the salted water to a boil. Drop the dumplings into the boiling water. Let them simmer for 15 to 20 minutes.

6. Drain the dumplings thoroughly and keep them warm in a slow (250°) oven while you prepare the Avgolemono Sauce. Or make the dumplings in advance and reheat them in the sauce.

Serves 4 to 6.

Malfatti cheese and spinach dumplings

In Italy, gnocchi were originally called ravioli, and in some places still are. Malfatti means "badly made" and perhaps are so called because they are not wrapped in dough, as one might expect in the case of ravioli. But they aren't wrapped because they are really gnocchi. Whatever you call them, these dumplings are easy to make and delicious. The spinach-cheese mixture is refrigerated overnight, so leave yourself plenty of time.

2   10-ounce packages frozen spinach*
2   teaspoons salt
1   pound fresh ricotta
2½ cups soft breadcrumbs
¼   cup grated Romano cheese
3   eggs, lightly beaten
½   cup finely chopped scallions (green tops included)
1   tablespoon finely chopped fresh basil or 2 teaspoons dry basil
½   cup chopped parsley
1   large garlic clove, finely chopped or put through press
    Pinch nutmeg
    Several grindings black pepper
    Flour to roll dumplings in
6–8 quarts of salted water

To serve

½ stick melted butter and freshly grated Parmesan cheese or a Tomato Sauce, pages 184–185

1. Place frozen spinach in a saucepan with 2 teaspoons of salt. Cover, and cook over low heat for about 15 minutes, or until completely thawed. Drain, squeeze out all the liquid, and chop fine.

2. In a large bowl, combine all the ingredients except the flour and water. Mix well. Cover and refrigerate overnight.

3. Form oval dumplings 3 inches long and about 1 inch in diameter. Roll each one in flour. Do not let them touch each other while they stand.

4. Bring the salted water to a boil. Drop the dumplings into the boiling water to form one layer. After they float to the surface, cook them for 4 minutes more.**

5. Lift out the cooked malfatti with a slotted spoon, letting them drain well. Place in a well-buttered ovenproof dish. Keep them warm in a slow (250°) oven while you finish cooking the dumplings.

6. To serve, pour melted butter over the malfatti and sprinkle with grated Paramesan cheese or tomato sauce.

Serves 6 to 8.

Notes and Variations

*1. If you wish to use fresh spinach, see Notes for gnocchi verdi on page 58 for preparation instructions.

**2. You may freeze malfatti after poaching. No need to defrost them. To serve, brush with butter, sprinkle with Parmesan cheese, and heat in 350° oven for ½ hour.

Malfatti in Tomato Sauce.

Flounder and Shrimp Quenelles

Fish quenelles, light as air, are one of the glories of French cooking. They are certainly a very elegant dumpling. The addition of shrimp to the flounder enriches the flavor. You may omit it if you like, and increase the flounder fillet by ¼ pound.

   1 *pound flounder fillets*
   ½ *pound raw shrimp*
   1 *cup water*
1½ *teaspoons salt*
   ½ *stick unsalted butter*
   1 *cup all-purpose flour*
   2 *eggs, plus 2 egg whites*
   ¼ *teaspoon nutmeg*
      Several grindings white pepper
   4 *tablespoons heavy cream, very cold*
      Flour for shaping quenelles
      Mushroom Sauce, page 182

1. Put the fish and shrimp through the finest blade of a meat grinder twice, or puree them in a food processor. Refrigerate the puree.

2. Bring the cup of water to a boil together with the salt and butter. When the butter has melted, add the flour all at once and beat with a wooden spoon over moderate heat until the mixture forms a mass and leaves the sides of the pan.

3. Off the heat, beat in the 2 eggs, one at a time, beating each one until it is incorporated completely. Then beat in the egg whites. Use either a wooden spoon or a food processor to do this. Remove the dough to a large mixing bowl.

4. Beat in the fish/shrimp puree along with the nutmeg and white pepper. Beat vigorously until everything is well blended. Cover the bowl and refrigerate for 2 to 3 hours, until the mixture is quite cold.

5. Beat in the tablespoons of heavy cream one at a time.

6. Flour your hands well, and keeping extra flour nearby, form ovals approximately 2 inches long and 1 inch thick by scooping out a rounded soupspoon of the mixture and tossing it lightly from floured hand to floured hand. Place on a well-floured baking sheet while you make the rest.

7. In a 10- or 12-inch skillet bring about 3 inches of water to a simmer. Gently slide the quenelles into the water and poach them, no more than 6 or 8 at a time, for 20 minutes. Do not let the water come to a boil. The quenelles will puff up, double in size, and turn over easily when they are done.

8. Remove them with a slotted spoon to a well-buttered baking dish and keep them warm in a slow (250°) oven until they are all done.

9. When ready to serve, coat them with Mushroom Sauce and serve with additional sauce passed separately.

Serves 4 as a main course or 6 as a first course.

Notes and Variations

Quenelles can be made a day or 2 ahead of time. Arrange all the poached quenelles in the buttered baking dish, brush with melted butter, cover, and refrigerate. Reheat in a 350° oven for 30 minutes.

Gefilte Fish

Gefilte means "stuffed" in Yiddish, and this refers to a traditional Jewish method of preparing freshwater fish such as pike or whitefish to give them more flavor. The fish was stuffed with a mixture of matzoh meal, herbs, and vegetables. Because freshwater fish tends to be extremely bony, another method evolved: The fish was filleted and ground together with the above ingredients, and stuffed back into the reserved skin, to make little oval pouches. Today gefilte fish is no longer stuffed; instead fillets of fish (preferably a combination of several different kinds) are ground together, seasoned, formed into ovals and poached in fish stock. The result is a delicious fish dumpling, a variation of quenelles, to be served cold in some of the jellied stock, along with very good horseradish.

Stock

    Fish trimmings, i.e., heads, skin, and bones, from 4 pounds of fish such as pike, whitefish, carp, haddock, or any other firm, white-fleshed fish
3 *onions, quartered*
2 *carrots, scraped and cut in large chunks*
2 *stalks celery, including some leaves, sliced*
    Several sprigs parsley
12 *black peppercorns*
1 *clove garlic, unpeeled*

Approximately 2 quarts water
1 *teaspoon sugar*
1 *additional carrot, scraped and sliced*
    Salt and pepper to taste

Dumplings

4 *pounds fillet of pike, whitefish, carp,*
  haddock, or other firm white-fleshed
  fish, preferably a combination of 2 or
  more varieties
1 *onion, sliced into chunks*
1 *clove garlic*
3 *large eggs, lightly beaten*
¼ *cup matzoh meal*
¼ *cup ice water*
2 *teaspoons salt*
  Several grindings black pepper

1. Put the fish heads, skin, and bones in a large kettle together with the onions, 2 carrots, celery, parsley, peppercorns, garlic, and about 2 quarts of water. The water should cover the trimmings. Bring to a boil, lower the heat, and simmer, covered, for 30 minutes.

2. Put the fish fillets through a meat grinder with the sliced onion and garlic clove. (A food processor may be used or even a blender if you do the fish a little at a time.)

3. Put the ground fish mixture in a bowl and add the eggs, matzoh meal, ice water, salt, and pepper. Mix well to blend. Cover the bowl and refrigerate.

4. Strain the fish stock to remove all vegetables and trimmings, and place the clear stock in a clean kettle. Add the sugar, additional carrot, and salt and pepper to taste. Simmer gently over low heat while you form the dumplings.

5. With wet hands, shape the fish mixture into egg-size ovals. Lower them into the simmering stock, cover, and simmer over low heat for 1½ hours.

6. Let the dumplings cool in the stock until they are room temperature. Remove to serving bowl and arrange them to your liking. Cover with carrot slices and pour fish stock over all. Cover and refrigerate overnight or for several hours until the stock has jelled.

7. Serve as main course or appetizer with grated horseradish.

Yield: About 16 to 20 gefilte fish.

Chicken Quenelles

Serve these light and delicate dumplings in your very best chicken broth for a truly elegant soup, or serve them as a separate course with a rich Madeira sauce, page 183.

½ cup milk
3 tablespoons butter
¼ teaspoon salt
1 cup all-purpose flour
1 egg
1 pound boneless chicken breast, finely ground
½ stick butter, softened to room temperature
2 egg whites
3 tablespoons chilled heavy cream
Salt and pepper to taste
Pinch nutmeg
2–3 quarts boiling water

1. Place the milk, 3 tablespoons of butter, and salt in a small saucepan. Bring to a boil, remove from heat, and add the flour all at once. Beat with a wooden spoon for 1 minute. Return to low heat and cook, stirring constantly, until the mixture forms a ball and leaves the sides of the pan.

2. Off the heat, beat in the egg with a wooden spoon until well blended. Remove to a large bowl.

3. Add the ground chicken, beating with a wooden spoon until mixed thoroughly. Then beat in the softened butter, egg whites, and heavy cream. Season with salt, pepper, and nutmeg.

4. Cover the bowl and place in the refrigerator for several hours, until the mixture is well chilled.

5. Shape the mixture into 2½-inch ovals.

6. Place the quenelles in a large skillet and pour over them just enough boiling water to cover. Poach over low heat (the water should barely simmer) for 20 minutes. Remove with a slotted spoon to a buttered baking dish. (The quenelles may be refrigerated for a couple of days at this point.)

7. To serve in soup, drop them into simmering broth for a few minutes before serving just to reheat, or brush with butter and reheat in the oven for 10 minutes.

Yield: About 18 to 20 quenelles.

Notes and Variations

You may drop the quenelles directly into simmering broth and cook for 20 minutes.

Albondigas Mexican meat dumplings

I read somewhere that the word "albondigas" comes from the Arabian meaning "to swim." Appropriate enough for these spicy, juicy meat dumplings swimming in chili-flavored sauce.

½ pound beef, ground
½ pound pork, ground
2 eggs, lightly beaten
2 slices stale bread, soaked in ½ cup milk
2 hard-boiled eggs, yolks and whites chopped
    separately
¼ cup ground almonds (optional)
⅛ teaspoon ground cloves
⅛ teaspoon cinnamon
½ teaspoon ground cumin
¼ teaspoon rosemary
1 teaspoon salt
  Several grindings black pepper
2 tablespoons chili powder (more or less
    depending on taste)
3 cups beef stock
2 tablespoons grated cheddar or other hard
    cheese

1. In a large bowl, mix together the beef, the pork, and the 2 raw eggs.

2. Squeeze excess milk from the bread and crumble onto the meat mixture.

3. Add the chopped egg yolks, ground almonds, cloves, cinnamon, cumin, rosemary, salt, and pepper. Mix well, and form into walnut-size balls.

4. Add the chili powder to the beef stock and bring to a boil.

5. Drop the albondigas into the boiling stock. Simmer for 30 minutes.

6. Preheat the oven to 350°.

7. Stir the chopped egg whites into the stock. Place the albondigas and stock in an ovenproof casserole and sprinkle with grated cheese. Bake for 20 minutes

Serves 4 to 6.

Turkey Albondigas

Leftover turkey can be transmogrified into dumplings swimming in thickened and reduced turkey stock. Make the stock from what is left of the turkey after you have picked off the meat. You may substitute chicken stock and/or leftover chicken for the turkey.

3 cups cooked turkey
3 slices bread, sprinkled with 6 to 7 tablespoons of the hot stock
3 eggs
1–2 garlic cloves, finely chopped or put through a garlic press
2 teaspoons salt
1 teaspoon ground coriander
1 teaspoon ground cumin
Several grindings black pepper
2 quarts turkey stock* or chicken stock
1 10-ounce package frozen kernel corn
¾ cup blanched almonds, finely ground
Chopped green chili peppers for garnish (optional)

1. Place the turkey meat in a bowl. Squeeze excess moisture from the bread and crumble it onto the turkey meat.

2. Put the turkey and bread through a meat grinder or food processor.

3. Add the eggs, garlic, salt, coriander, cumin, and black pepper. Mix well.

4. Shape the mixture into walnut-size balls.

5. Bring the turkey or chicken stock to a boil. Drop the albondigas into the boiling broth. Simmer for 10 minutes.

6. Remove with slotted spoon and set aside.

7. Boil the broth for another 30 minutes to reduce and thicken it. Add the corn and ground almonds, and return the albondigas. Heat through and serve in bowls garnished with chili peppers, if you wish.

Serves 6 to 8.

Notes and Variations

*To make the stock, pick the meat off the bird. Put the turkey carcass into a large pot and cover with water. Add an onion, a carrot, a stick of celery, some parsley, thyme, and a bay leaf. Simmer for 2 or 3 hours. Cool, strain, and season.

Konigsberger Klops dumplings in caper sauce

A variety of meatballs seems to exist in almost every national cuisine. Germany's contribution, Konigsberger klops, are very light and delicate. Poached and sauced, they make a most elegant dish.

2 *pounds beef, finely ground*
2 *tablespoons butter*
2 *large onions, finely chopped*
4 *large slices of bread, cubed and soaked in*
   1 *cup evaporated milk*
4 *anchovy fillets, finely chopped*
2 *eggs, lightly beaten*
½ *teaspoon salt*
   Several grindings black pepper
1 *tablespoon lemon juice*
1 *quart beef broth*
⅔ *cup dry white wine*

Caper Sauce

2 *tablespoons butter*
2 *tablespoons flour*
1–1½ *cups reserved hot beef broth*
1 *teaspoon Dijon mustard*
1 *egg yolk*
   Juice of 1 lemon
¼ *cup drained capers*
   Good pinch cayenne pepper
2 *tablespoons finely chopped parsley*

1. Place the ground beef into a large bowl.

2. In a large skillet, melt the butter. Sauté the onions until very light brown, stirring frequently.

3. Crumble the milk-soaked bread onto the meat. Add the sautéed onions and chopped anchovy fillets and mix thoroughly.

4. Add the eggs, salt, pepper, and lemon juice. Mix well. Taste and adjust seasoning.

5. Form the meat mixture into walnut-size balls.

6. Combine the beef broth and wine in a 10- or 12-inch saucepan. Bring to a boil.

7. Drop the klops into the boiling broth. Cover and simmer about 12 minutes. Test one to see if it is done.

8. Remove the klops with a slotted spoon to an ovenproof baking dish and keep in a warm (250°) oven while you make the caper sauce. Reserve 1½ cups of the broth.

9. To make the sauce, melt the butter in a skillet and stir in the flour. Cook over low heat, stirring frequently, to make a golden roux, about 12 minutes.

10. Add the reserved beef broth, stirring until smooth. Stir in mustard.

11. Beat the egg yolk in a bowl and add a tablespoon or 2 of the hot sauce. Add the egg yolk to the sauce, stirring constantly. Do not allow to boil or sauce will curdle. Add lemon juice, capers, and cayenne. Taste and adjust seasoning if necessary. Pour the caper sauce over the klops and serve, garnished with parsley.

Serves 6.

Meatloaf Dumpling to serve with caper sauce

Try this recipe once and you may never cook meatloaf any other way. The giant dumpling is so moist and juicy it truly rivals any other ground meat dish I know. The meat is shaped into a large ball and completely encased in cheese cloth to keep its shape while it cooks.

1½ pounds beef, ground
½ pound pork, ground
1 hard roll, soaked in ½ cup buttermilk
1 medium onion, finely chopped
1 garlic clove, finely chopped or put through garlic press
1 small stick celery, finely chopped
2 tablespoons finely chopped fresh dill
2 tablespoons finely chopped parsley
½ teaspoon hickory-smoked salt
1 teaspoon paprika
1 teaspoon dry mustard
½ teaspoon thyme
1½ teaspoons salt
Several grindings black pepper
3 eggs, lightly beaten
Flour for dredging cheesecloth
6–8 quarts salted water

1. Place the ground meat into a large bowl. Crumble the roll onto the meat. Add the other ingredients, except for the flour and water, and mix well, kneading with your hands, until very well blended.

2. Cut a large square of cheesecloth several layers thick. Dredge it well with flour.

3. Shape the meatloaf mixture into a large ball and place it onto the cheesecloth. Gather up the cheesecloth and tie securely at the top.

Place meatloaf dumpling in center of flour-dredged cheesecloth.

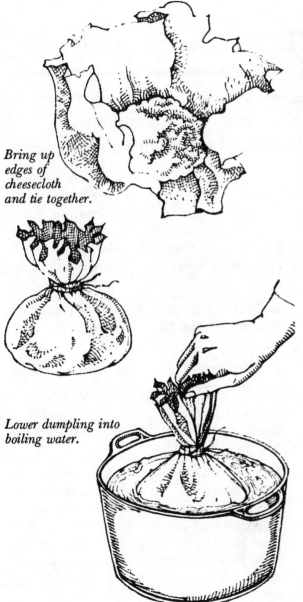

Bring up
edges of
cheesecloth
and tie together.

Lower dumpling into
boiling water.

4. Bring the salted water to a boil. Slide the wrapped meatloaf dumpling into the boiling water. Cover and simmer for 1½ hours.

5. The only tricky part in the whole procedure is removing the hot cheesecloth from around the dumpling. An extra pair of hands and good kitchen scissors are a big help.

6. Serve with Caper Sauce, page 52.

Serves 6.

Ricotta Gnocchi

delicate, light dumplings from Italy

Traditionally these gnocchi are served as a first course. But they could happily accompany a roast or a stew. They could also be poached in a light beef or chicken broth and served floating in a bowl of soup.

½ stick butter, softened to room temperature
½ pound ricotta, pressed through a sieve into a bowl
2 eggs, lightly beaten
4 tablespoons freshly grated Parmesan cheese
6–8 tablespoons all-purpose flour, plus additional flour for shaping gnocchi
1 teaspoon salt
Several grindings white pepper
Pinch nutmeg
6–8 quarts of salted water

To serve
½ stick melted butter
Freshly grated Parmesan cheese

1. Put the softened butter into a medium bowl. Beat in the ricotta until thoroughly blended. An electric blender works nicely here, but a whisk or a fork will do just as well.

2. Beat in the eggs, the grated Parmesan cheese, and the flour to form a smooth mixture.

3. Add salt, pepper, and nutmeg. Taste and adjust seasoning, if necessary.

4. Cover the mixture and put into the freezer for ½ hour, or refrigerate 2 to 3 hours or overnight.

5. Dust your hands with flour and have flour nearby so that you can keep your hands well floured as you work. Scoop a tablespoon of the mixture and plop it in your hand. Toss it lightly from floured hand to floured hand and shape it into an oval. If the mixture is too soft, add

another tablespoon or 2 of flour. Place the gnocchi on well-floured waxed paper on a cookie sheet as they are formed.

6. Bring the salted water to a boil. Gently slide 6 to 8 gnocchi into the boiling water. Cook for 2 to 3 minutes after the gnocchi float to the surface. Repeat until all are done.

7. Remove the cooked gnocchi with a slotted spoon and place in a buttered ovenproof dish.*

8. When all are done, pour melted butter over them and sprinkle with grated Parmesan cheese.** Place in a 350° oven for 10 minutes to melt the cheese. Serve.

Serves 4 as a main course, 6 as a side dish or first course.

Notes and Variations

*1. Gnocchi can be frozen after poaching. To serve, defrost and reheat in oven.

**2. Or sauce them with one of the Tomato Sauces, pages 184–186.

Ricotta gnocchi.

Gnocchi Verdi   spinach and ricotta gnocchi

1   10-*ounce package frozen leaf spinach**
1   *teaspoon salt*
2   *tablespoons butter*
1   *medium onion, finely chopped*
2   *tablespoons unsmoked ham, finely chopped*
      (optional)
1   *cup fresh ricotta*
⅓   *cup all-purpose flour and additional flour*
      for shaping gnocchi
1   *egg*
1   *cup freshly grated Parmesan cheese*
      Several grindings black pepper
      Pinch nutmeg
6–8   *quarts salted water*

To serve

½   *stick melted butter*
      Freshly grated Parmesan cheese

1. Place the frozen spinach into a saucepan with the salt. Cover, and cook over low heat for about 15 minutes or until completely thawed. Drain, squeeze out the liquid, and chop finely.

2. In a medium skillet, melt the butter and sauté the onion until golden brown. Add the chopped spinach and ham, and continue to sauté for 5 minutes, stirring frequently.

3. Transfer the spinach mixture to a mixing bowl. Add the ricotta, ⅓ cup flour, egg, Parmesan cheese, pepper, and nutmeg. Stir well and taste for salt. Cover and refrigerate the dough for several hours or overnight.

4. Shape the dough into dumplings the size of a plum. Keep your hands well floured as you work. Arrange the gnocchi on a cookie sheet lined with waxed paper.

5. Bring the salted water to a boil. Drop 6 to 8 gnocchi into the water. Cook for 5 minutes after the gnocchi rise to the surface. Repeat until all are cooked.

6. Remove the cooked gnocchi with a slotted spoon and place in buttered baking dish.** Pour melted butter over the gnocchi and sprinkle with Parmesan cheese.

7. Before serving, place gnocchi verdi into a hot (400°) oven for about 5 minutes to melt the cheese.

Yield: About 24 plum-size gnocchi; serves 4 to 6.

Notes and Variations

*1. You can, of course, use fresh spinach instead of frozen. You will need 1 pound. Remove the stems and wash well under cold running water. Make sure that all the grit is removed. Drain well and cook the spinach in a large, covered pot with no more water than adheres to the leaves and a little salt, until wilted and tender. Drain, squeeze out excess moisture, and chop finely.

**2. The gnocchi may be frozen after poaching. Arrange in buttered ovenproof dish and cover tightly. To serve, remove from freezer, dot with butter, and reheat in 350° oven.

3. Serve with one of the Tomato Sauces, pages 184–186.

Potato Gnocchi

Velvety smooth, rich, and satisfying, potato gnocchi are undoubtedly the most exquisite of the potato dumplings. Serve them as a first course or on their own for lunch.

2 *pounds medium potatoes*
2 *egg yolks*
1½ *teaspoons salt*
Several grindings black pepper
1 *cup all-purpose flour*
6–8 *quarts salted water*

To serve

1 *stick melted butter and freshly grated Parmesan cheese, or a Tomato Sauce, pages 184–186 or Pesto, page 187*

1. Scrub the potatoes, but do not peel. Boil them in water to cover for 30 minutes or until done. Drain and peel.

2. Puree the potatoes through a food mill or potato ricer into a large bowl.

3. Add the egg yolks, salt, pepper, and enough of the flour to make a soft dough. You may need more or less flour depending on the moisture content of the potatoes.

4. Divide the dough into 4 equal parts. Roll each part into a sausage about ¾ inch thick. Cut off 1-inch pieces.

5. Press one side of each dumpling against the tines of a fork.

6. Bring the salted water to a boil. Drop the gnocchi into the boiling water to form one layer. Cook for 10 to 12 minutes.

7. Remove the gnocchi with a slotted spoon and place them in a well-buttered baking dish. Pour a little of the melted butter or tomato sauce over the gnocchi to keep them moist. Place in a slow (250°) oven until all are done and you are ready to serve them. Serve with grated cheese and the melted butter, tomato sauce, or pesto.

Serves 6 to 8.

The
Filled
Dumplings

Notes on Filled Dumplings

I will not hesitate to say that filled dumplings are a luxury in this day and age. Not a luxury in terms of expense, as say, caviar or filet mignon, but a luxury in terms of time. Each individual dumpling must be stuffed by hand, and for some people, these simple hand operations are a drudgery. But when friends ask *me* why I bother, I rarely need to do more than to serve them some homemade ravioli, piroshki, or pelmeni, and the reason is clear.

The basic filled dumpling is elegantly simple: flour and water, sometimes an egg or two, perhaps a little shortening to make a dough. Roll the dough out and cut it into circles or squares. Place a little well-seasoned filling in each, close the edges tightly, sealing with a little water if necessary, and make shapes that are traditional, or not. Boiled, fried, or steamed, filled dumplings are some of the most appealing and popular foods in the world.

Most of the dumplings in this section can be made way ahead of time and frozen. I generally put aside one rainy Sunday every month for "putting up" a huge batch of dumplings. I do it when I *feel* like doing it and to hell with deadlines. Naturally, I reward myself that night with a wonderful dinner—and freeze the rest. Then, for weeks, unexpected guests are welcomed and well fed.

Here are a few tips on making filled dumplings:

1. *The Dough*

Many people are timid about working with dough, and yet if you keep a few simple rules in mind, there is nothing the least bit tricky about making the wrappings for the filled dumplings in this section.

You will need a large, uncluttered work area with a smooth surface on which to roll your dough, as well as a sturdy rolling pin. (I prefer the European kind of rolling pin that is reminiscent of a truncated broom handle and has no ball bearings or other mechanical parts.)

I recommend all-purpose white, unbleached flour unless otherwise noted in the recipe. Aside from the flour called for in the individual recipes, you will need to keep additional flour nearby to dust your work surface and your hands. Keep in mind that sometimes you will need to use a little more or a little less flour or water than specified in the recipes because flours vary and are affected by the humidity in the air. Continue to add a little flour or water until the dough seems right to you.

The dough is made by mixing the solid and liquid ingredients together until they form a mass. Then it is kneaded. Most of the recipes call for the dough to be kneaded until it feels smooth and satiny. Once you have done this a few times, you will know exactly what this means. The dough should feel slightly damp, with a texture that is resilient and feels alive. If all of this still sounds confusing, forget it, and knead the dough for an honest 8 to 10 minutes and all will be well.

After the dough is kneaded and before it is rolled out, it should be allowed to rest, well covered, of course, so that it doesn't dry out. The rest period "relaxes" the dough and allows you to roll it out to the thinness desired. Let it rest for at least 30 minutes; it can happily stay in the refrigerator for as long as a day, allowing you to time things to your convenience.

You will find it easier to roll out the dough if you divide it in half,

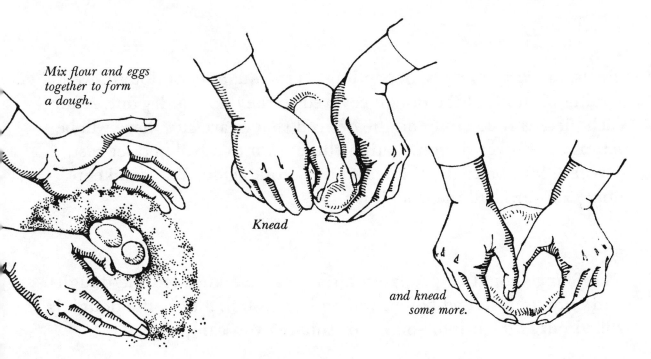

Mix flour and eggs together to form a dough.

Knead

and knead some more.

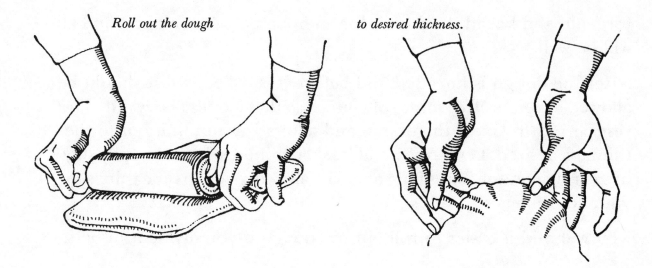

Roll out the dough *to desired thickness.*

thirds, or even quarters, depending on the quantity of dough. Keep waiting portions of the dough covered so they do not dry out. After each piece is rolled out and the desired shapes are cut, there will be scraps of leftover dough. Gather these up into a ball and let rest, covered, for about 10 minutes, and roll out again. You can keep doing this until all the dough is used.

2. *The Filling*

The filling should be prepared after you have kneaded the dough and put it to rest, and before rolling it out, so that once the dough is rolled out and cut into rounds or squares you can proceed immediately to filling and shaping the dumplings. While you roll the dough out, keep the filling in the freezer. This is not essential, but a firmer filling is easier to work with.

3. *Making the Dumplings*

As you make the dumplings you will need to arrange them so that as they wait to be cooked they won't touch each other and stick together or stick to the surface. Have several large baking sheets or trays that you have dusted with flour close by and arrange the dumplings on them. If your kitchen feels warm and humid, it may be best for the dumplings to wait in the refrigerator, lest they become sticky and shapeless. If your kitchen is cool and dry, however, the dumplings can sit out for a while until you are ready to cook them.

4. *Freezing the Dumplings*

Freeze the dumplings after they are filled but before they are cooked. To freeze them properly, have a large wire cake rack handy and arrange the dumplings on the rack so that they don't touch each other. Place the rack uncovered in the freezer. This allows the dumplings to freeze quickly all around. When they're frozen through, just dump them into a plastic bag. The bag should be sealed tightly and marked with the date and contents. Don't defrost the dumplings before cooking, but proceed with the cooking directions in the recipe, adding a few minutes to the cooking time.

Fried Pork Dumplings from China

These are the dumplings most often served in Chinese restaurants—they are deservedly popular and somehow seem doubly pleasing when served at home.

Dough for the wonton skins

- 1 *cup all-purpose flour, plus additional flour for shaping wonton*
- 6 *tablespoons cold water*

Filling

- 6 *dried Chinese mushrooms*
- ¾ *pound ground pork*
- ¼ *pound raw shrimp, shelled, deveined, and finely chopped*
- ⅓ *cup finely chopped bamboo shoots*
- 1 *egg, lightly beaten*
- 1 *tablespoon dry sherry or Chinese rice wine*
- 2 *tablespoons soy sauce*
- 1 *teaspoon freshly grated ginger root*
- 2 *teaspoons cornstarch*
- 1 *teaspoon salt*
- ¼ *teaspoon monosodium glutamate (optional)*
- ½ *cup peanut or vegetable oil for frying*
- 1 *cup chicken stock*

1. Soak the mushrooms for 30 minutes in warm water. Drain and squeeze dry. Remove the stems and chop the caps finely.

2. Mix the flour and water together. Remove to a floured board and knead for about 5 minutes, until the dough feels satiny. Roll into a ball, cover, and let rest for 30 minutes or longer.

3. Meanwhile, put the mushrooms, pork, shrimp, and remaining filling ingredients into a bowl and mix together well. Chill in freezer while you make the wrappings.

4. Divide the dough into 4 parts. Cover 3 of them, and roll the fourth part into a sausage about 8 inches long. Cut the dough sausage into 6 pieces, and form each of these into a small ball. Flatten each ball with the heel of your hand, and then roll it out into a circle about 3 inches in diameter and about $1/16$ inch thick. Don't worry if it is not a perfect circle. Once the dumplings are

Place filling in center of round dough wrapper.

Bring two sides together making small pleats in the dough.

Seal the edges.

stuffed, they will look pretty much alike. Repeat with the remaining dough.

5. Remove the filling from the freezer and place about 1 tablespoon of filling into the center of each circle. Bring 2 sides together at the top and pinch together. Flatten the bottom. What you are after is a kind of small boat look, rather than a crescent shape. Tuck the other ends, pleating them in the middle, and pinch all the edges together to seal well. (The dumplings can be frozen at this point for future use.)

6. Heat ½ of the oil in a large skillet or wok over high heat. Place half of the dumplings into the skillet, pinched sides up, and fry until the bottoms are just brown. Add ½ cup of the chicken stock, cover, and cook over moderate heat for 10 minutes. Remove cover and

cook another minute or so until all the liquid is evaporated. Remove to a platter and keep them warm while you cook the second batch in the remaining oil and chicken stock.

7. Serve accompanied by small bowls filled with a Soy Dipping Sauce, page 178 and/or Duck Sauce, page 181, and/or Mustard-Vinegar Sauce, page 180.

Yield: About 24 dumplings.

Notes and Variations

1. These dumplings can also be boiled or steamed, see page 73. If you have any dumplings left over, you can reheat them by sautéeing them in a little oil.

2. Ready-made wonton skins may be used, but this dough gives a more tender wrapping.

Fried Wonton

Wonton, the most famous of Chinese dumplings, is usually served in soup, but it is even better fried and served with sweet and sour sauce, page 179.

Wonton skins*

- 2 *cups all-purpose flour plus additional flour for shaping wonton*
- 1 *egg, lightly beaten*
- ¾ *cup cold water*
- 1 *teaspoon salt*

Filling

- ½ *bunch watercress, picked over, dead leaves and tough stems removed*
- ½ *pound ground lean pork*
- ½ *pound raw shrimp, shelled, deveined, and finely chopped*
- 4 *water chestnuts, finely chopped*
- 1 *egg, lightly beaten*
- 1 *tablespoon dry sherry or Chinese rice wine*
- 2 *tablespoons soy sauce*
- 1 *tablespoon cornstarch*
- 1 *tablespoon water*
- ½ *teaspoon salt*
  - *Several grindings black pepper*
- ¼ *teaspoon monosodium glutamate (optional)*
- 3–4 *cups vegetable oil for deep frying*

1. Mix together the ingredients for the wonton skins. Knead to form a stiff dough and remove to a floured board. Knead for 5 to 10 minutes until the dough feels smooth and satiny. Roll the dough into a ball, cover, and let rest for 30 minutes.

2. Meanwhile, plunge the watercress into a large kettle of boiling water for 30 seconds. Drain, and run under cold water. Squeeze dry and chop fine.

3. Mix together the pork and shrimp in a bowl. Add the watercress and remaining filling ingredients. Mix well.

4. Knead the dough for a minute or 2 and roll it out to a thickness of $1/16$ inch and cut into 3-inch squares or 3-inch rounds. (The square shape is more traditional for wonton.) Keep skins covered so that they do not dry out.

5. Place about a teaspoon of filling into the center of each wonton wrapping. Bring up 2 sides of the skin and pinch

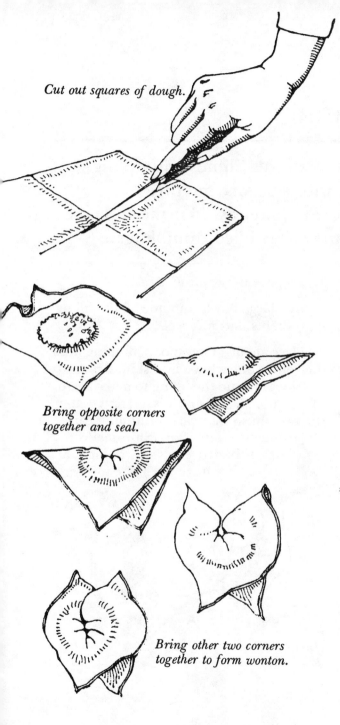

Cut out squares of dough.

Bring opposite corners together and seal.

Bring other two corners together to form wonton.

together all around the filling. Bring the other 2 ends together and pinch firmly together. Use a little water to make sealing easier. (The wonton can be frozen at this point for future use.)

6. Heat the vegetable oil to 360°, in a deep-frying kettle or wok.

7. Fry the wontons, about 10 at a time, for 3 minutes or until golden brown. Drain on absorbent paper and keep warm in a slow (250°) oven while you fry the remaining wonton. Wonton can be kept warm in the oven for up to an hour, or made ahead and reheated in a medium (350°) oven for 20 minutes

8. Serve with Sweet and Sour Sauce, page 179.

Yield: About 40 to 50 wonton.

Notes and Variations

*1. Half a package of ready-made wonton skins may be used.

2. To serve the wonton in chicken broth, cook them in 7 to 8 quarts of boiling salted water until they float to the top. Serve in bowls of hot chicken broth.

Shui-Mai steamed pork dumplings

Shui-mai are perhaps the prettiest of all the Chinese dumplings—
little cups of steamed dough filled with a savory mixture
of pork and shrimp. They are, however, quite easy to make and take
less time to prepare than most of the other filled dumplings.

Wonton skins

24–30 *ready-made 3-inch round wonton*
skins or 1 *recipe wonton skins, page* 70

Filling

½ *pound ground pork*
½ *pound raw shrimp, shelled, deveined, and*
coarsely chopped
¼ *cup finely chopped bamboo shoots*
4 *scallions, finely chopped (green tops*
included)
3 *tablespoons chicken broth*
1 *tablespoon soy sauce*
1 *teaspoon cornstarch*
1 *tablespoon dry sherry* or *Chinese rice wine*
1 *teaspoon salt*
1 *teaspoon sesame oil*
½ *teaspoon sugar*
¼ *teaspoon monosodium glutamate (optional)*

1. Prepare the wonton skins.

2. In a large bowl, combine all the filling ingredients and mix well.

3. Place about 1 tablespoon of filling into the center of each wonton skin. Bring up the sides around the filling to make a cup. Make little pleats as necessary, and flatten the bottom so that each dumpling can stand on its own. (Shui-mai can be frozen at this point for future use.)

Place filling
in center
of round
dough wrapper.

4. Place the shui-mai on a lightly oiled plate, making sure they do not touch each other.

5. Steam* them for 20 minutes.

6. Serve with one of the Chinese dippings sauces on pages 178–179, and/or Mustard-Vinegar Sauce, page 180.

Yield: About 24 to 30 shui-mai.

Notes and Variations

Shui-mai look especially nice when topped with minced Chinese mushrooms, minced water chestnuts, and a couple of frozen peas. Garnish *before* steaming.

*To steam, arrange the dumplings on a lightly oiled plate, but do not let them touch each other. If you own a Chinese bamboo steamer and a wok, then you can steam several plates at one time. Pour approximately 2 inches of boiling water into the wok, set the plates in the steamer and set the steamer in the wok. Cover the steamer and cook over moderate heat. If you do not have a Chinese steamer, you can easily improvise. Pour about 2 inches of water into a large (6 quarts), wide (at least 10 inches in diameter) pot. Place a can or small inverted bowl or anything else that works into the pot and put the plate on that. The idea is to lift the plate to just above the water level. Cover the pot and cook over moderate heat.

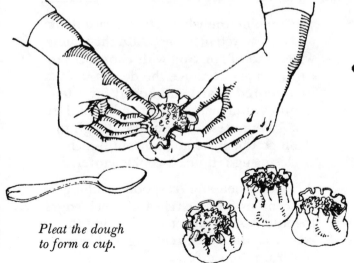

Pleat the dough to form a cup.

Shui-mai in a steamer.

Steamed Translucent Chinese Dumplings with two fillings

I've been enjoying these dumplings in New York's Chinatown for years. Like most people, I guess, it never occurred to me until recently that these delicate-looking dumplings could be easily made at home. Wheat starch and rice flour are the secret of the unusual translucent skins. Both ingredients can be obtained in Oriental markets and in some health food stores. Make the fillings on page 76 before the dough, since the shrimp must be chilled and the crabmeat must be stir-fried and cooled before the dumplings can be filled.

Dough

- 2 cups wheat starch
- ½ cup rice flour, plus additional flour for shaping dumplings
- ¼ cup cornstarch
- 2⅔ cups boiling water
- 1 tablespoon vegetable oil

1. Combine the wheat starch, rice flour, and cornstarch in a bowl. Add the boiling water and oil, mixing with chopsticks to form a mass. Remove the dough to a well-floured board and knead for a few minutes until firm. Roll into a ball and let rest 10 minutes. Roll out the dough to $1/16$-inch thickness and cut out 3-inch circles using a floured cookie cutter.

2. Place a heaping teaspoon of filling in the center of each circle and pinch edges together to seal. Start by pinching the center of the half-circle edges. Then pinch up the sides.

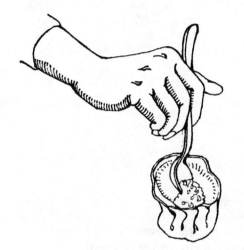

3. Place the dumplings on a greased plate that will go in the steamer. Refrigerate them until ready to cook. (Dumplings may be frozen at this point for future use.)

4. Steam them for 10 minutes over boiling water as described on page 73.

5. Serve hot with one of the sauces on pages 178–181, or with Chinese hot oil and white vinegar.

Yield: About 40 to 50 dumplings.

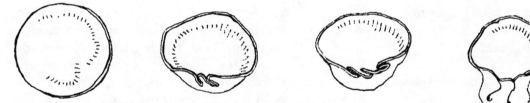

Make small pleats on one edge of a round dough wrapper to form a pocket.

Place filling in pocket and bring edges together to seal.

Shrimp Filling for Translucent Dumplings

1 *pound fresh raw shrimp, shelled, deveined, and finely chopped*
3 *scallions, finely chopped (green tops included)*
4 *water chestnuts, finely chopped*
1 *teaspoon soy sauce*
1 *teaspoon salt*
 Several grindings black pepper
1 *tablespoon vegetable oil*

Combine all the ingredients in a bowl, cover, and refrigerate for at least 1 hour.

Crabmeat Filling for Translucent Dumplings

3 *dried Chinese mushrooms*
3 *tablespoons peanut oil*
1 *tablespoon fresh ginger root, grated*
½ *pound fresh crabmeat (or one 7½ ounce can), flaked*
¼ *teaspoon salt*
 Several grindings black pepper
¼ *teaspoon sugar*

1. Soak the mushrooms in warm water for ½ hour. Drain and squeeze them dry. Remove the stems and chop the caps finely.

2. Heat the oil in a wok or skillet. Cook the ginger, mushrooms, and crabmeat over high heat, stirring continuously, for 3 minutes. Add salt, pepper, and sugar. Cook 1 minute more. Cool mixture before stuffing dumplings.

Egg Rolls

Skins

20–30 *ready-made, 6- inch-square, egg roll skins* or*
4 *cups all-purpose flour, plus additional flour for shaping egg rolls*
1 *teaspoon salt*
2 *eggs, lightly beaten*
1–1½ *cups water*

1. Combine flour and salt in a bowl and add the eggs and enough water to form a soft dough.

2. Remove the dough to a well-floured board and knead for about 10 minutes until dough is smooth and elastic.

3. Cover and let rest for 30 minutes.

4. Cut dough into quarters and roll out, one section at a time, to ⅛-inch thickness. Cut into 6-inch squares. Flour each square well and stack them one on top of the other. Cover and refrigerate while you prepare the filling on the following page. Continue with remaining dough until all are done.

Yield: About 24 skins.

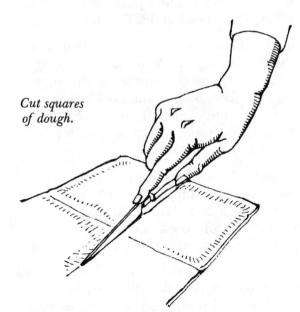

Cut squares of dough.

Filling for Egg Rolls

  8 *dried Chinese mushrooms*
  ½ *pound fresh bean sprouts***
  4 *tablespoons vegetable oil*
  ½ *pound ground lean pork*
  ¼ *pound chicken breast, skinned, boned,*
     and shredded
  ½ *pound shrimp, shelled, deveined, and*
     coarsely chopped
  ½ *cup shredded bamboo shoots*
  ½ *cup chicken broth*
  2 *tablespoons dry sherry* or *Chinese rice*
     wine
  1 *tablespoon sugar*
1½ *teaspoons salt*
  1 *tablespoon soy sauce*
  4 *teaspoons cornstarch, dissolved in 4*
     teaspoons water
  1 *cup shredded scallions (green tops*
     included)
  1 *teaspoon sesame oil*
  1 *egg, lightly beaten, for glazing*
  4 *cups peanut or vegetable oil for deep*
     frying

1. Soak mushrooms in warm water for 30 minutes. Drain and squeeze out moisture, remove stems, and shred the caps.

2. Rinse bean sprouts and pick over them to discard husks. Drain and pat dry.

3. Heat 2 tablespoons of the vegetable oil in a wok or frying pan and add the pork. Cook over high heat for 1 minute, stirring, or until the pork has lost its pink color. Add the chicken and cook stirring, until chicken loses its pink color, about 1 minute. Then add shrimp and continue cooking over high heat, stirring, for 1 minute more. Remove pork, chicken, and shrimp to a bowl and set aside.

4. To the same wok or frying pan add the remaining 2 tablespoons of vegetable oil and heat, then add the mushrooms and bamboo shoots, and cook, stirring, for 1 minute over high heat. Add the bean sprouts and cook, stirring, for 1 minute.

5. Add chicken broth, sherry, sugar, salt, and soy sauce and cook, stirring, until it reaches a boil. Add the dissolved cornstarch and cook, stirring, for 1 minute until mixture thickens.

6. Return pork, chicken, and shrimp to the wok or frying pan and stir. Stir in scallions and sesame oil. Remove to bowl and set aside to cool.

To make the egg rolls

1. Place filling mixture in a sieve or colander to drain off excess liquid.

2. Keep the skins covered with a slightly damp cloth so that they do not dry out while you work.

3. Place 1 skin at a time so that 1 corner is pointing toward you. Place about 2 tablespoons of filling just below the center of the skin.

4. Fold over the front corner of the skin to cover the filling.

5. Use a pastry brush to paint the remaining 3 sides with the beaten egg.

6. Fold over the side flaps to form an envelope and roll from bottom up to form a cylinder. Make sure it is tightly sealed with the egg glue.

To fry the egg rolls

1. Heat the 4 cups of peanut or vegetable oil to 360°.

2. Fry 4 to 6 egg rolls at a time until they are golden, about 3 minutes.

3. Remove and drain on absorbent paper.

4. Serve as part of a meal, or as an appetizer, accompanied by Duck Sauce, page 181 and Mustard-Vinegar Sauce, page 180.

Yield: About 24 egg rolls.

Notes and Variations

*1. Substitute prepared Shanghai Spring Roll skins for egg roll skins for a more delicate wrapping.

**2. You may substitute canned bean sprouts if necessary. Use one 1-pound can of sprouts. Drain and place in a bowl, cover with cold water, and refrigerate for 2 hours. Rinse, drain, and pat dry.

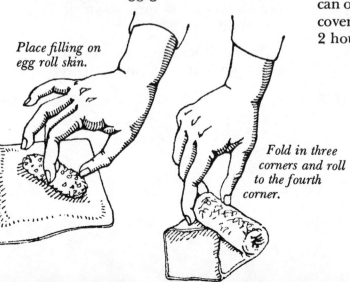

Place filling on egg roll skin.

Fold in three corners and roll to the fourth corner.

Seal.

Pearl Balls
a Chinese meatball dumpling coated with pearly rice

Pearl balls are not exactly a filled dumpling because they are simply covered with a layer of glutinous rice, nor are they dropped dumplings because they are steamed rather than dropped into a cooking medium. However, they are impressive looking, very easy to make, and delicious. Pearl balls are good as appetizers, as a main course, or as part of a larger dumpling assortment.

⅔ cup glutinous rice*
4 dried Chinese mushrooms
1 pound ground lean pork
3 scallions, finely chopped (green tops included)
½ teaspoon grated fresh ginger root
½ teaspoon sugar
3 tablespoons cornstarch
2 tablespoons soy sauce
1 tablespoon dry sherry or Chinese rice wine
½ teaspoon baking soda
¼ teaspoon monosodium glutamate (optional)

1. Cover the rice with 1⅓ cups cold water and let soak for 2 hours. Drain, and spread out on paper toweling to dry.

2. Meanwhile, soak the mushrooms in warm water for 30 minutes. Drain, squeeze them dry, and remove the stems. Chop the caps finely.

3. In a large bowl, mix together the mushrooms and all the remaining ingredients.

4. Shape the mixture into walnut-size balls. It helps if your hands are wet.

5. Roll the balls in the rice to coat.

6. Arrange the balls on lightly oiled plates, and steam over boiling water for 30 minutes. (See steaming instructions on page 73.

7. Serve with one of the Soy Dipping Sauces, page 178, and/or the Mustard-Vinegar Sauce, page 180.

Yield: About 16 pearl balls. Make them smaller for appetizers; then you get more.

Notes and Variations

*1. Glutinous rice is also known as Sweet Rice and Sticky Rice, and is available in Oriental food stores.

2. Add a little raw, minced shrimp to the mixture.

Mandoo   Korean dumplings

Mandoo, Korea's contribution to dumpling cuisine, owes its unusual texture to the use of bean sprouts and sauerkraut in the filling. The result is a dumpling that is tangy and delicious.

Skins

1 *package wonton skins, round or square,* or *1 recipe for wonton skins, page* 70.

Filling

½ *pound bean sprouts*
1 *pound ground chuck*
½ *pound sauerkraut, rinsed under running water, drained, moisture squeezed out, and coarsely chopped*
1 *bean curd cake,* drained*
4 *scallions, finely chopped (green tops included)*
1 *garlic clove, finely chopped or put through garlic press*
1 *egg, lightly beaten*
2 *teaspoons cornstarch*
1 *teaspoon sugar*
1 *teaspoon grated fresh ginger root*
2 *teaspoons salt*
  Several grindings black pepper
⅛ *teaspoon monosodium glutamate (optional)*
1 *tablespoon toasted sesame seeds***

1. Prepare the wonton skins.

2. Plunge bean sprouts into boiling water for 2 minutes. Drain and chop coarsely.

3. In a large bowl, mix together all ingredients for the filling.

4. For round wonton skins, put a heaping spoonful of filling into each center, bring edges together and seal to make a crescent. For square wonton skins, put a heaping teaspoonful of filling into each center, bring top and bottom edges together to seal, then bring sides around to overlap and seal. The final shape is somewhat triangular. (Mandoo can be frozen at this point for future use.)

5. Mandoo may be fried, boiled, or steamed. To fry, follow instructions for fried wonton on page 70. To boil, drop the mandoo into 7 to 8 quarts of boiling salted water and cook until they float to the top. Cook no more than 1 layer at a time. To steam, follow the instructions for shui-mai on page 73.

6. Serve with Cho-Chang Sauce, page 180, or one of the Chinese sauces.

Yield: About 60 to 80 mandoo.

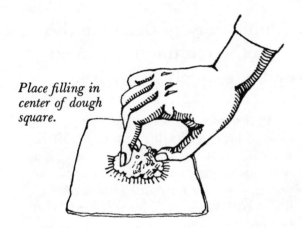

Place filling in center of dough square.

Notes and Variations

*1. Also known as Tofu, it is available in Oriental and health food stores.

**2. To toast sesame seeds, place a small skillet over medium heat, add sesame seeds, and stir with chopsticks or wooden spoon. Watch carefully. They toast in minutes.

3. You can substitute a bunch of watercress for the bean sprouts. Remove tough stems and plunge into boiling water for 1 minute. Rinse under cold water, drain, squeeze dry, and finely chop.

Fold opposite edges together and seal.

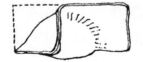

Fold corners down to form a triangle.

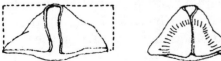

Manty
Uzbek steamed lamb-filled dumplings

As the dumpling made its way from East to West in the ancient history of cuisine, one of the first stops was the place in Central Asia that is now the Uzbek Republic. The similarities of manty to the classic Chinese dumplings are obvious, although the use of mint leaves and yogurt as garnishes makes it a uniquely local dish.

Dough*

3 cups all-purpose flour, plus additional
 flour for shaping manty
1½ cups water
1 teaspoon salt

Filling

1½ pounds ground lean lamb
1½ cups finely chopped onions
1 teaspoon salt
 Several grindings black pepper
1 stick cold butter

 Approximately ⅓ cup fresh mint leaves,
 finely chopped
1 cup unflavored yogurt

1. In a medium bowl, mix together the flour, water, and salt to make a stiff but workable dough. Place the dough on a well-floured board and knead until the dough feels smooth and satiny. Shape into a ball. Cover and let rest for at least ½ hour.

2. Meanwhile, in a bowl, mix together the lamb, onions, salt, and pepper. Knead with your hands until they are well combined.

3. Roll out the dough until very thin, about $^1/_{16}$ inch. Cut out circles with a 4-inch cookie cutter (a 1-pound coffee can works well, too).

4. Put 2 to 3 tablespoons of the filling, topped with a ¼-inch slice of butter into the center of each circle. Bring up the sides, and pinch them together at the top to close the pouch.

5. Place the manty on a lightly oiled plate, making sure that they do not touch each other. Steam over boiling water for 15 minutes as described on page 73.

6. Serve sprinkled with mint leaves and a dollop of yogurt.

Yield: About 20 to 22 manty.

Notes and Variations

*1. Or use ready-made round wonton skins.

2. Fresh, minced dill can be substituted for the mint leaves.

3. Serve one of the Vinegar-Soy Sauces, page 178, along with or instead of the yogurt.

Chebureki

Deep-fried, lamb-filled Tatar dumplings from the Caucasus, chebureki are best eaten with your hands. The procedure is to bite into one corner, and slurp (yes, very loudly) the juices, so they won't drip out and be lost. A plate of chebureki, a jug of good, cheap red wine, sliced tomatoes, and fresh scallions, dipped in coarse salt make a wonderful outdoor meal on a summer evening.

Dough

- 3 *cups all-purpose flour, plus additional flour for shaping chebureki*
- 1 *egg*
- ¾ *cup water*
- 1 *teaspoon salt*

Filling

- 1½ *pounds ground lean lamb*
- 1 *medium onion, finely chopped*
- 2 *tablespoons finely chopped coriander*
- ¼ *cup finely chopped parsley (the flat-leaf variety, if possible)*
- 2 *teaspoons salt*
  Several grindings black pepper
- 4 *tablespoons water, or more*
- 3–4 *cups vegetable oil for deep frying*

1. In a bowl, mix together the flour, egg, water, and salt to make a stiff but workable dough. Place on a well-floured board, and knead until the dough feels smooth and satiny. Form into a ball. Cover and let rest for 30 minutes.

2. Meanwhile, mix together the filling ingredients, adding enough water to make the filling juicy, but not soupy. Taste for seasoning, and adjust if necessary. A *lot* of black pepper is good here.

3. Divide the dough in half. Cover one half and roll out the other to ⅛-inch thickness. Use a 3½- or 4-inch cookie cutter, or a 1-pound coffee can to cut out circles.

4. Fill each circle with about 2 tablespoons of filling. Fold the circle in half to make a half moon and seal the edges, moistening them with a little water if necessary.

5. Heat the vegetable oil to 360°.

6. Drop the dumplings into the hot oil and fry a few at a time, until golden brown. Drain on absorbent paper and serve immediately.

Yield: About 20 to 22 chebureki.

Notes and Variations

My mother also makes chebureki filled with lean ground beef. She substitutes dill for the coriander. Everything else is the same. Good, too.

Cut out circles of dough with a coffee can.

Place filling in center of dough circle.

Fold in half

and seal the edges.

Pelmeni meat-filled Siberian dumplings

Perhaps pelmeni was the original frozen dinner. Siberian housewives have always kept sacks of frozen pelmeni in the snow surrounding their homes. Pelmeni are boiled in water and served on their own with a variety of sauces, or boiled in beef broth and served in the soup garnished with lots of dill. Make them ahead and store in the freezer. When you are ready to have some, simply drop frozen pelmeni into boiling, salted water.

Dough

4 cups all-purpose flour, plus additional flour for shaping pelmeni
3 eggs, lightly beaten
1 cup warm water
1½ teaspoons salt

Filling

¾ pound ground beef
¼ pound ground pork
1 medium onion, very finely chopped or grated
1 garlic clove, put through a garlic press
2 tablespoons finely chopped fresh dill*
1 teaspoon salt
Several grindings black pepper
2 tablespoons water
7–8 quarts salted water

To serve

½ stick melted butter
Lemon wedges
Sour cream (if you like) or
Mustard-Vinegar Sauce, page 180.

1. In a bowl, mix together flour, eggs, water, and salt to make a firm dough. Remove to a well-floured board and knead until the dough feels smooth and satiny, about 10 minutes. Form the dough into a ball. Cover and let rest for ½ hour.

2. Meanwhile, mix together beef, pork, onion, garlic, dill, salt, pepper, and 2 tablespoons of water. Refrigerate until ready to use.

3. Divide the dough in half. Cover one half and roll out the other until it is ⅛ inch thick. Use a 2½- or 3-inch round cookie cutter to cut out rounds.

4. Place about 1 teaspoon of filling on each round. Bring 2 edges together to seal in the filling. Then pinch the 2 corners together. Dip your fingers in a small bowl of water while you are doing this so that the edges are well sealed. (The pelmeni can be frozen at this point for future use.)

5. Bring the salted water to a boil and drop in about 10 to 12 pelmeni at a time. Cook for 8 minutes or until pelmeni float to the top of the water. Repeat until all are done.

6. Remove with a slotted spoon to a well-buttered baking dish. Pour a little melted butter over them and keep them warm in a slow (250°) oven until all are done.

7. Serve with lemon wedges, sour cream, or Mustard-Vinegar Sauce.

Yield: About 70 to 80 pelmeni.

Notes and Variations

*Omit if you cannot find fresh dill.

Meat-Filled Piroshki from Russia

Because the meat in these piroshki is first boiled along with bones, vegetables, and seasonings to make a beef broth, and then ground and seasoned for filling these delicious yeast-raised dumplings, the entire process, from start to finish, takes quite a long time. I usually do it slowly over 2 days. The end result is definitely worth it—a pot of savory beef broth, and a great many delicious piroshki.

Broth

2 *pounds chuck*
4 *marrow bones*
2 *carrots, scraped and coarsely chopped*
1 *parsnip, trimmed and cut into chunks*
3 *celery stalks, trimmed and sliced into chunks*
  Several sprigs parsley
1 *onion, peeled and stuck with 4 cloves*
1 *clove garlic, unpeeled*
12 *peppercorns*
  Approximately 5 quarts water

1. Place all the broth ingredients in a kettle with just enough water to cover. Bring to a boil and reduce to a simmer. Simmer, covered, for 3 hours, skimming regularly until all the scum is removed.

2. Remove the beef and reserve the liquid. Strain the broth and allow to cool in refrigerator. Once it is cold remove all the fat from the surface.

Yield: About 3 quarts beef broth (unsalted).

Dough

1½ cups milk
4 tablespoons (½ stick) butter
1 envelope dry active yeast
⅓ cup warm water
3 tablespoons sugar
4–5 cups unbleached flour
1 tablespoon salt
2 eggs, lightly beaten, plus
 an additional egg for brushing filled
 piroshki

1. Scald the milk in a saucepan and remove from heat. Add the butter and let stand until butter melts and milk is just warm.

2. Sprinkle the yeast over the warm water along with a pinch of the sugar. Stir to dissolve the yeast and let stand in a warm place for about 10 minutes.

3. Place 4 cups of flour in a large bowl along with the sugar and salt. Make a well in the center and add the milk and butter mixture, the yeast mixture, and the eggs. Use a wooden spoon to combine the flour with the liquid ingredients into a sticky dough.

4. Remove the dough to a well-floured board and start kneading, adding up to 1 more cup of flour, until the dough feels smooth and is no longer sticky.

5. Gather the dough into a ball and place into a warm, buttered large bowl. Cover with plastic wrap and let rise in a warm place until double in bulk (about 1½ hours). Punch the dough down and let it rise again for another hour.

6. While the dough is rising, prepare the filling.

Filling for piroshki

⅓ cup vegetable oil
2 large onions, finely chopped
  Reserved, cooked beef from the broth, put
    through a food grinder or very finely
    chopped
  Salt and pepper to taste
2 tablespoons finely chopped fresh dill

Heat the oil in a large skillet. Add the onions and cook until they turn light brown. Add the beef and blend well. Season with salt and pepper and add the dill. Remove to a bowl and allow to cool before using.

Making the piroshki

1. After the second rising, place the dough on a lightly floured board and knead for a few minutes. Divide the dough into 4 parts. Work with 1 part at a time and keep the remainder covered.

2. Roll the dough you are working with into a long rope. Cut this into pieces approximately the size of Ping-Pong balls. Roll each piece into a ball and then flatten into a 3-inch circle. Place about a tablespoon of filling in the center of each circle and bring up the sides to enclose the filling, forming a crescent. It is traditional to flatten the bottom of the crescent so the piroshki stand up like small boats, but do not worry about this if it seems complicated.

3. Preheat oven to 350°. Place the formed piroshki on a greased baking sheet, leaving at least 2 inches of space between them as they will expand as they bake.

4. Brush the piroshki with a beaten egg and bake for 25 minutes or until they have all turned a deep, golden brown. Serve them hot, warm, or cold.

Yield: About 45 to 50 piroshki.

Meat-filled piroshki.

Notes and Variations

1. The piroshki may be frozen after they are formed and before baking. I arrange them on inexpensive, disposable aluminum baking sheets or lasagna pans, cover tightly with aluminum foil and freeze. When you are ready to bake them, remove from freezer, brush with beaten egg, and pop directly into 350° oven. Increase the baking time by 5 or 10 minutes.

2. The filling may be made a great deal richer by adding a pound of mushrooms finely chopped, that have been sautéed in ½ stick butter until soft, into the meat mixture.

3. A couple of hard-boiled eggs, chopped, may be added to the meat mixture.

Mushroom Piroshki from Russia

These piroshki are much quicker and easier to make than the yeast dough, meat-filled variety because of the pastry crust and a filling that takes only minutes to prepare. They are delicious served as an appetizer or as an accompaniment to soups.

Dough

3½ *cups all-purpose flour, plus additional flour for shaping piroshki*
1 *teaspoon baking powder*
1 *teaspoon salt*
1 *tablespoon sugar*
1 *stick cold butter*
2 *eggs*
1 *cup sour cream*

1. Sift flour, baking powder, salt, and sugar into a bowl. Cut the butter into the flour until the mixture is the consistency of oatmeal.

2. Beat the eggs together with the sour cream until smooth, then add to the flour mixture. Blend to form a mass and remove to a floured board.

3. Knead for a few minutes to make a smooth dough. Form into a ball, cover, and chill in the refrigerator for 1 hour.

Filling

½ stick butter
¾ pound mushrooms
6 scallions, finely chopped (green parts included)
1 tablespoon flour
3 tablespoons sour cream
2 hard-boiled eggs, coarsely chopped
3 tablespoons chopped fresh dill
  Salt
  Several grindings black pepper
1 egg, lightly beaten, for glazing

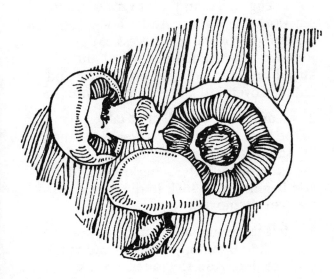

1. Melt the butter in a skillet and add the mushrooms and scallions. Sauté for 10 minutes.

2. Sprinkle the flour over the mushroom mixture and continue sautéeing, stirring constantly with a wooden spoon, for 1 minute.

3. Add sour cream, stir to blend, and remove from heat.

4. Off the heat, add the chopped eggs, dill, and salt and pepper to taste.

5. Divide the dough in half, keeping one half cold while you work with the other. Roll the dough out on a floured board to a thickness of ¼ inch.

6. Cut the dough into 3-inch rounds. Place 1 tablespoon of filling in the center of each round and fold into a crescent shape, pinching the edges to seal. Continue rolling, cutting, and filling until all the filling has been used.

7. Preheat oven to 400°.

8. Place the piroshki on a buttered baking sheet and brush them with the beaten egg.

9. Bake for about 20 minutes, until they are golden.

Yield: About 36 to 40 piroshki.

Vareniki with sauerkraut filling

Vareniki, the Ukrainian national dumplings, are made with a great variety of fillings. (See page 169, for vareniki filled with cheese and fruit.) Try serving these unusual dumplings with a fried or broiled garlic sausage. Or accompany them with thick slices of grilled bacon.

Dough

2 *cups all-purpose flour, plus additional flour for shaping vareniki*
1 *egg*
½ *cup milk*
1 *teaspoon salt*
2 *egg whites*

Filling

½ *stick butter*
1 *pound sauerkraut, rinsed under cold running water, squeezed dry, and finely chopped*
1 *medium onion, finely chopped*
½ *teaspoon sugar*
½ *teaspoon salt*
   Several grindings black pepper
½ *cup dry white wine*
2 *tablespoons sour cream*
7–8 *quarts salted water*

To serve

½ *stick butter*
2 *medium thinly sliced onions*

1. In a bowl, mix together the flour, whole egg, milk, and salt to make a stiff but workable dough. Add a few tablespoons of water if necessary. Remove to a well-floured board and knead until the dough feels smooth and satiny. Cover and let rest for 30 minutes.

2. Meanwhile, melt about 1 tablespoon of the butter in a heavy skillet, and sauté the sauerkraut over low heat for about 5 minutes, or until the sauerkraut is dry and beginning to stick to the bottom of the pan. Remove it to a bowl.

3. Melt the remaining butter in the skillet. Add the chopped onion and sauté until golden. Add the sauerkraut, sugar, salt, pepper, and wine. Turn heat as low

as possible. Cover tightly and braise for 45 minutes. Check occasionally to see that all the liquid has not evaporated and the sauerkraut is not burning.

4. Remove from heat. Stir in the sour cream and taste for seasoning. Let cool completely before you stuff the vareniki.

5. Divide the dough in half. Cover one half and roll the other out to a thickness of ⅛ inch. Use a 3-inch cookie cutter to cut out as many circles as possible. Repeat with remaining dough.

6. Beat the egg whites until frothy. With a pastry brush, coat each circle with the beaten egg whites.

7. Place approximately 1 tablespoon of filling on each circle. Press edges together to make a half moon. Make sure the edges are well sealed. (Vareniki can be frozen at this point for future use.)

8. Bring the salted water to a boil and drop in the vareniki, about 10 at a time. Simmer until they float to the top.

9. Remove with a slotted spoon and place in a buttered ovenproof dish. Keep them warm in a slow (250°) oven until all are done.

10. Sauté the sliced onions in the ½ stick butter until they are brown and beginning to crisp.

11. Serve vareniki covered with the fried onions.

Yield: About 50 to 60 vareniki.

Uszki Polish dumplings filled with mushrooms

Uszki, the Polish version of pelmeni and vareniki, are really called "uszki postne", meaning "Lenten dumplings", to distinguish them from the meat-filled variety. They are stuffed with dried imported Polish mushrooms, and make a peasant dish to rival any in "haute cuisine." Serve uszki on their own, as an accompaniment to roasts and stews, or in soup.

Dried Polish mushrooms are sold in specialty stores and are worth the additional expense, as well as the trouble it takes to find them.

Dough

3½ cups all-purpose flour, plus additional
    flour for shaping uszki
2 eggs
1 cup water
1 teaspoon salt

Filling

½ pound dried imported Polish mushrooms*
1 onion
1 clove
  Pinch of salt
1 stick butter
1 medium onion, finely chopped
¼ teaspoon thyme
¼ pound fresh mushrooms, finely chopped
½ cup fresh breadcrumbs, from dark bread
    if possible
1 tablespoon finely chopped fresh dill
1 teaspoon salt
  Several grindings black pepper
7–8 quarts salted water

To serve

½ stick melted butter
  Sour cream (optional)

1. Simmer the dried mushrooms with the onion, clove, and salt in a quart of water for 1 hour.

2. In a bowl, mix together flour, eggs, water, and salt to make a stiff but workable dough. Remove to a floured board and knead until the dough feels smooth and satiny, about 5 to 10 minutes. Form the dough into a ball. Cover and let rest while you make the filling.

3. Drain the simmered mushrooms and wash them carefully. (If you wish to reserve the broth for soups or sauces, strain it through cheesecloth.) Discard the onion and clove. Chop the mushrooms finely.

4. Melt the butter in a skillet. Add the chopped onion and thyme and sauté until soft.

5. Add all the mushrooms, bread crumbs, dill, salt, and lots of pepper. Sauté, stirring often, for 15 minutes. Taste for seasoning and adjust if necessary. Let cool before using.

6. Cut the dough into 4 parts. Cover 3 parts while you roll out the fourth on a well-floured board until it is very thin, about $1/16$ inch thick. Cut out circles or squares with a 2-inch cookie cutter.

7. Place 1 teaspoon of filling on each circle. Pinch the edges together to form a half moon. Make sure the edges are well sealed. Repeat until all dough and filling are used. As you make the uszki, place them on a well-floured cookie sheet. Make sure the dumplings do not touch each other. Cover the uszki with a flour-dredged towel. They can stand for several hours in a cool dry place. (Uszki can be frozen at this point for future use.)

8. Bring the salted water to a boil and drop in the uszki, about a dozen at a time. Simmer until they float to the top.

9. Remove with a slotted spoon and place in a buttered ovenproof dish. Keep warm in a slow (250°) oven until all are done.

10. Before serving, pour melted butter over the uszki, and pass a bowl of sour cream, if you like.

Yield: About 80 to 90 uszki.

Notes and Variations

*1. If you cannot find imported Polish mushrooms, substitute ½ pound of other dried mushrooms. Supermarkets usually carry Italian dried mushrooms. Do not use Chinese mushrooms, however: The flavor is too strong.

2. Instead of boiling the uszki, sauté them in butter until golden brown on both sides. This is good for cold, leftover uszki as well.

Kreplach and three fillings

Grandmothers seem to make the best kreplach, but that should not deter you from trying your hand at these famous Jewish dumplings.

Dough

- 2 cups all-purpose flour, plus additional flour for shaping kreplach
- 2 large eggs
- ½ teaspoon salt
- 1½ tablespoons water

In a bowl, combine the dough ingredients. Mix to form a firm dough. Remove dough to a well-floured board and knead until it feels smooth and satiny. Cover and let rest for 30 minutes, while you make one of the fillings.

Meat filling

- 2 tablespoons butter or rendered chicken fat
- 1 medium onion, finely chopped
- ½ pound ground beef
- 1 teaspoon salt
  Several grindings black pepper

1. In a skillet melt the butter or chicken fat. Add the onions and sauté, stirring occasionally, until they are light brown.

2. Add the ground beef and cook, stirring, until meat is no longer pink.

3. Add the salt and pepper, mix well, and remove from heat. Let cool before filling the kreplach.

Cheese filling

- 2 cups dry cottage cheese, farmer cheese, or pot cheese
- 2 egg yolks
- 1 tablespoon sour cream
- ½ teaspoon salt

Combine all ingredients and mix with a wooden spoon until well blended.

Kasha filling

1 cup kasha*
1 egg, lightly beaten
2 cups boiling water
2 teaspoons salt
2 tablespoons butter or rendered chicken fat
1 medium onion, finely chopped
½ cup finely chopped mushrooms
½ cup ground beef
Several grindings black pepper

1. Put the kasha into a heavy (cast-iron) pot or frying pan. Add the egg and cook over medium heat, stirring constantly, until the grains are separate and dry. Add the boiling water and 1 teaspoon of the salt. Cover and cook over very low heat for 30 minutes.

2. Melt butter or chicken fat in a skillet. Add the onion and sauté until it is light brown.

3. Add the mushrooms and beef. Cook, stirring, until beef is no longer pink.

4. Remove from heat, add the cooked kasha, remaining salt, and pepper. Mix well. Let cool before filling kreplach.

Making the kreplach

1. Divide the dough in 2 parts. Cover one half and roll out the other on a well-floured board until it is about ⅛ inch thick. Repeat with remaining dough.

2. Cut the dough into 3-inch squares. Place about 1 tablespoon of filling onto the center of each square. Fold into a triangle and seal.

3. Bring 7 to 8 quarts of salted water to a boil, and drop the kreplach into it, about 8 to 10 at a time. Simmer until they float to the top and drain. Repeat until all are done.

4. Serve meat kreplach in soup or separately with lots of melted butter and grated horseradish; cheese kreplach covered with melted butter and passed with sour cream and a variety of jams; kasha kreplach in soup or separately with melted butter.

Yield: About 40 to 50 kreplach.

Notes and Variations

*Kasha, more correctly known as buckwheat groats, can be found in most supermarket and health food stores.

Ravioli and a choice of four fillings

Ravioli are the most famous of the Italian filled dumplings. They are prepared throughout Italy with a great variety of fillings. One theory about the origins of ravioli is that they were originally made as a convenient and tasty way to use leftovers. Leftover stews, pieces of meat and vegetables were ground up, seasoned, and used as stuffing for ravioli. This should certainly encourage you to experiment with making your own fillings, as well as to try your hand at preparing the recipes below.

Dough

2 *cups all-purpose flour, plus additional*
   flour for shaping ravioli
½ *stick butter*
1 *teaspoon salt*
1 *cup boiling water*

1. Put the flour into a bowl. Add the butter in thin slices, then the salt.

2. Stir in the cup of boiling water, and mix together with a large fork or chopsticks. When the mixture has formed a mass, take it out of the bowl and place on a well-floured board and knead it until it becomes a soft, sticky dough that is rather easy to work and roll out. Form the kneaded dough into a ball and place it back in the bowl. Cover with plastic wrap so that it does not dry out while it rests. Prepare one of the following fillings.

Two cheeses filling

4 *ounces freshly grated Parmesan*
6 *ounces grated Provolone*
½ *cup heavy cream*
3 *eggs, lightly beaten*
  Several grindings black pepper
  Pinch nutmeg
1 *teaspoon dry basil* or *2 tablespoons finely chopped fresh basil*

In a medium bowl, mix together all the ingredients. Taste and correct for seasoning. Refrigerate until ready to use.

Four cheeses filling

1 *cup ricotta, put through a sieve into a bowl*
4 *ounces freshly grated Parmesan*
2 *ounces freshly grated Romano*
4 *ounces grated Gruyère or Emmentaler*
1 *egg, lightly beaten*
½ *cup heavy cream*
2 *tablespoons finely chopped parsley (preferably the flat-leafed variety)*
  Several grindings black pepper

In a medium bowl, mix together all ingredients. Taste, and correct for seasoning. If too dry, add a little more cream. Refrigerate until ready to use.

Parsley and ricotta filling

1½ *cups ricotta*
1 *cup freshly grated Parmesan*
⅓ *cup finely chopped parsley (preferably the flat-leafed variety)*
1 *egg, lightly beaten*
  Several grindings black pepper

In a medium bowl, mix together all the ingredients. Taste and correct for seasoning. Refrigerate until ready to use.

Veal filling

½ stick butter
1 medium onion, finely chopped
½ pound ground veal
1 egg, lightly beaten
¼ cup freshly grated Parmesan
¼ cup breadcrumbs, freshly made, if possible
¼ cup finely chopped parsley
   Several grindings black pepper
   Salt to taste

1. Melt the butter in a skillet. Add the onion and sauté for about 5 minutes. Add the veal and cook until the meat is no longer pink, stirring constantly.

2. Remove from heat and stir in the egg, cheese, breadcrumbs, and seasonings. Taste and add more salt and pepper, if necessary. Let cool completely before stuffing the ravioli.

Making the ravioli

1. Clear a large work area and flour the surface well. Keep the flour nearby to dust the work surface and hands as you work. Prepare a lightly floured tray or cookie sheet to put the formed ravioli on.

2. Cut the dough in half. Leave half in the bowl and cover. Cut the other half in half again. Roll each piece into a large rectangle about as thin as a penny. Cut the 2 rectangles into strips about 3 inches wide.

3. Place teaspoonfuls of filling in mounds along one strip, spacing them at least 2 inches apart. Cover with another 3-inch wide strip. Press down on the dough around each mound of filling. Repeat with remaining dough.

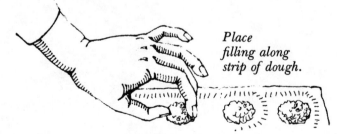

Place filling along strip of dough.

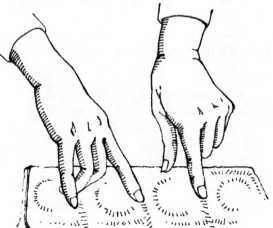

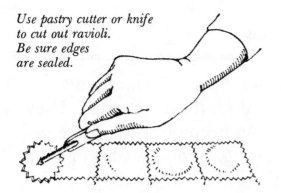

Use pastry cutter or knife to cut out ravioli. Be sure edges are sealed.

4. Using a 2½-inch round cookie cutter, a pastry wheel, or even a knife, cut out each round or square of ravioli. Make sure the edges are well sealed and that the filling is not leaking out. Place the sealed ravioli on the prepared tray and cover with a kitchen towel that has been well dredged with flour. The ravioli can wait for several hours before they are cooked. Turn them over every once in a while so that they dry evenly. (The ravioli can be frozen at this point for future use.)

5. Bring 6 to 8 quarts of salted water to a boil and drop in 6 to 10 ravioli at a time. Cook 1 minute more after they rise to the surface.

6. Remove with a slotted spoon and place them in a warm bowl that has been filmed with melted butter. Pour a little melted butter over the ravioli and keep them warm while you cook the rest. Pour melted butter over each batch of new arrivals.

7. Serve with grated Parmesan cheese or one of the Tomato Sauces, pages 184–186.

Yield: About 50 ravioli.

Notes and Variations

1. Try deep frying the ravioli. Heat 4 cups of vegetable oil to 360°. Deep fry ravioli about 2 minutes or until golden brown. Remove with slotted spoon and drain on absorbent paper. Very crisp on the outside, melted cheese on the inside. Delicious and good with drinks. Serve immediately.

2. Leftover ravioli are good when sautéed in butter. I have a friend who makes them a day ahead just to be able to eat them that way.

3. Good in soup.

4. You can vary the fillings endlessly, using your imagination and what you have on hand. The veal stuffing is delicious with some cooked Italian sausage added to it. Add a little chopped, cooked spinach to any of the stuffings. Invent your own—use any leftover cooked meat or poultry. Add some onion cooked in butter, moisten with a little cream and seasoning.

Capelletti small, filled pasta "caps"

Do not make capelletti when you are in a hurry. It takes time, perhaps a whole afternoon, to shape and fill these tiny caps. They are, however, wonderful to have on hand in the freezer. I like to make them with a friend, leisurely, chatting, sipping a glass of wine. The end result, of course, amply justifies the time spent.

Dough

3 cups all-purpose flour, plus additional
   flour for shaping capelletti
3 eggs
2 tablespoons olive oil
½ cup warm water
1 teaspoon salt

Mix flour, eggs, olive oil, water, and salt together to make a firm dough. Knead on a well-floured board for about 10 minutes until the dough feels smooth and satiny. Form into a ball, cover, and let rest for 1 hour.

Filling

½ stick butter
¼ pound lean pork, diced into ½-inch cubes
¼ pound chicken breast, skinned and boned
   and diced into ½-inch cubes or ¼
   pound veal, diced into ½-inch cubes
4 tablespoons finely chopped unsmoked ham
1 cup fresh ricotta
1 cup freshly grated Parmesan
1 egg, lightly beaten
¼ teaspoon nutmeg
½ teaspoon salt
   Several grindings black pepper
6–8 quarts salted water

1. Melt 2 tablespoons of the butter in a skillet and add the pork cubes. Cook, stirring, for 15 to 20 minutes, until pork is cooked through. Remove to a bowl.

2. Melt the remaining 2 tablespoons butter in the skillet and cook the chicken or veal cubes for 6 or 7 minutes. Add to the pork.

3. Traditionally the meat should then be chopped by hand with a sharp knife; this does give it a more interesting consistency. Chop it very fine. Or put the meats through a meat grinder.

4. Add the chopped ham to the pork and chicken or veal mixture, then the cheeses, egg, and seasoning. Mix well and let cool completely before using.

Making the capelletti

1. Divide the dough in 3 or 4 parts and roll out 1 part at a time, until very thin (less than ⅛ inch thick). Cut the dough into 20 1-inch squares or use a 2-inch round cookie cutter to cut out rounds.

2. Stuff each square or round with ½ teaspoon of filling. If you are making squares, bring two points together to make a triangle. Seal the edges well by dipping your fingertips into a little water, if necessary. Then bring the other two points together, forming a little cap. Treat the circles similarly.

3. Place the capelletti on a well-floured baking sheet, and when the sheet is filled up, cover with a kitchen towel that has been well dredged with flour.

4. Let them dry 1 hour or longer before cooking. They can wait as long as a day, if your kitchen is cool and dry.

5. Bring the salted water to a boil. Drop the capelletti into the boiling water, about 1 dozen at a time, and cook for about 12 minutes. Remove with slotted spoon to a buttered ovenproof dish, moisten with a little melted butter, and keep them warm in a slow (250°) oven until all are done and ready to serve.

6. Serve with more melted butter and freshly grated Parmesan cheese or one of the Tomato Sauces on pages 184–186.

Yield: About 180 to 200 capelletti.

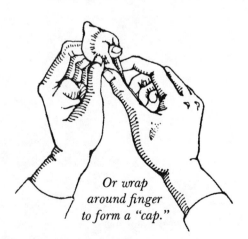

Or wrap around finger to form a "cap."

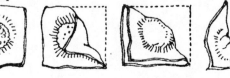

Place filling in center of dough square. *Bring two opposite corners together and seal the edges.* *Bring other two corners together.*

Kroppkakor
Swedish filled potato dumplings

While these dumplings are delicious with any roast or stew, they are especially good served with a good homemade applesauce and a green salad.

Dough

1½ *pounds potatoes*
 ¾ *cup flour, plus additional flour for shaping kroppkakor*
 1 *egg plus 1 egg yolk, lightly beaten*
 ½ *teaspoon salt*
    Several grindings black pepper

1. Peel and quarter the potatoes and boil them in salted water until they are tender. Drain, steam them dry, and put them through a food mill or sieve. Let them cool.

2. Combine 1½ cups of potatoes with the flour, eggs, salt, and pepper to make a smooth dough. Cover and let rest while you make the filling.

Filling

      3 *tablespoons salt pork, finely chopped*
     ⅓ *cup boiled ham, finely chopped*
      1 *small onion, finely chopped*
     ⅛ *teaspoon ground cloves*
3 *to* 4 *cups vegetable oil for deep frying*

To serve

      Melted butter and chopped parsley

1. In a small skillet, render the fat from the salt pork, add the boiled ham and the onion. Sauté until the onion is light brown. Stir in the cloves and let cool.

2. Roll the dough out to a thickness of ¼ inch on a well-floured surface. Use a 2-inch round cookie cutter to cut out rounds in the dough.

3. Place a heaping teaspoonful of the ham mixture in the center of half the rounds, and top with the remaining rounds, pressing the edges together. Roll into balls.

4. Heat vegetable oil to 360° and fry the kroppkakor a few at a time until they are golden. Drain on absorbent paper.

5. Top with melted butter and chopped parsley and serve.

Yield: About 1 dozen dumplings.

Apricot Dumplings

Usually fruit-filled dumplings are served as a separate course, either for dessert, breakfast or lunch. These apricot dumplings should be served as a delicious tangy side dish with your special roasts, stews, or chicken.

Dough

    2 *medium-size potatoes*
    1 *cup beer* or *water*
    ¾ *stick butter, cut in small pieces*
    1 *teaspoon salt*
    1 *cup flour*
    4 *eggs*
    1 *teaspoon sugar*
    ¼ *teaspoon baking powder*

Filling

10–12 *small fresh apricots* or *canned whole apricots, pitted*
    Approximately 7 to 8 quarts salted water

To serve

    ½ *cup bread crumbs sautéed in ½ stick butter*

1. Boil the potatoes until tender. Drain and push through a food mill or sieve. Let cool.

2. Bring the beer, butter, and salt to a boil, and boil gently until the butter has melted.

3. Pour in the flour all at once and beat with a wooden spoon until the dough forms a mass and leaves the sides of the pan.

4. Off the heat, beat in the eggs, one at a time, beating until completely blended. (If you have a food processor, transfer the dough to the food processor bowl and beat in the eggs one by one, using the steel blade.)

5. Beat in the potatoes, sugar, and baking powder.

6. Remove to a well-floured board and roll the dough out to a thickness of

⅛ inch. Cut into rounds with a
2½-inch cookie cutter.

7. Place an apricot in the center of each
round and bring up the dough to enclose
the apricot. Roll into a ball and dust with
flour.

8. Bring the water to a boil. Drop the
dumplings into the boiling water and
simmer until they rise to the top. Remove
with a slotted spoon and arrange them in
a buttered ovenproof dish.

9. Pour buttered breadcrumbs over
the apricot dumplings and bake in a
375° oven until golden brown. Serve
immediately.

Yield: About 10 to 12 dumplings.

Notes and Variations

1. The apricot dumplings can be made
ahead up to the point when they go into
the oven. Then they can wait until you
are ready for them.

2. Try prunes as filling. Poach them in a
little white wine to soften them. Proceed
as for apricots. Good with roast pork.

Jorge's Argentine Empanadas

My friend Jorge Castello tells me that in Argentina these empanadas are made on Sunday when "nobody wants to cook." They are, in fact, quite easy to make. Serve them any way you like. A couple of empanadas with a glass of wine or beer make a very satisfactory light meal. Add a green salad or sliced tomatoes or even a bowl of good soup, and you have a feast.

Dough

3 *cups all-purpose flour*
⅓ *cup melted lard*
1 *cup boiling water*
1 *teaspoon salt*

1. Measure the flour into a large bowl and add the melted lard, the boiling water, and the salt. Use a large fork or chopsticks to mix together into a mass.

2. Remove to a well-floured board and knead for 1 minute or so to form a ball. Cover and let rest for 10 to 15 minutes. Do not refrigerate; the dough is easier to roll out while still warm.

3. Cut the dough in half. Cover one half while you roll out the other half. Roll out the dough to the thickness of a quarter (it should not be too thin) and use a 2-pound coffee can to cut out circles. Stack the circles on a plate, one on top of the other. Proceed to roll and cut out the rest of the dough, gathering up the scraps and rolling them out again. When all the circles have been cut out, refrigerate them until you are ready to use them.

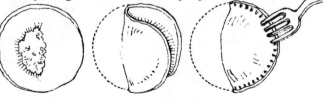

Place filling in center of dough.　*Fold in half and seal the edges with the tines of a fork.*

Filling

4 tablespoons olive oil
1 medium onion, finely chopped
1 clove garlic, finely chopped
½ pound ground beef
1 sweet red pepper, seeded and chopped or a
    green pepper if red is not available
2 teaspoons ground cumin
1 teaspoon paprika
1 teaspoon salt
    Several grindings black pepper
    Good pinch of cayenne pepper (optional)
⅓ cup green olives, chopped
4 tablespoons raisins, soaked in sherry
    (optional)
2 tablespoons pignola (pine nuts) (optional)
3 hard-boiled eggs, chopped
3–4 cups vegetable oil for deep frying

1. Heat the olive oil in a large skillet, add the onion and garlic and cook over medium heat until just soft. Add the beef and chopped pepper and cook, stirring with a wooden spoon to break up the meat, until the beef has lost all red color. Stir in the cumin, paprika, salt, black pepper, and cayenne.

2. Remove from heat and add the olives, raisins, and pignola nuts along with the eggs. Stir well and taste for seasoning. Let cool before using.

3. Have a small bowl of water at hand while you fill and seal the empanadas. Place 2 to 3 tablespoons of filling in the center of each circle. Dip a finger in water and moisten all the edges of the circle. Bring edges together to form a half moon, and seal by pressing down on the edges with the tines of a fork.

4. Heat oil to 360° and fry the empanadas 5 or 6 at a time for about 8 minutes or until golden brown. Remove and drain on absorbent paper. By the time all the empanadas are fried, the first ones will have cooled off just enough to eat.

Yield: About 16 to 18 empanadas.

Notes and Variations

1. I have found that the empanadas freeze best after they have been completely cooked. Freeze them after they have cooled. To serve, simply pop them into a 350° oven for about 25 minutes.

2. Jorge tells me that it is customary to sprinkle the empanadas with a little sugar just before serving. I've tried it and liked it.

The Fritters

Notes on Fritters

Call them frittas, frittelle, beignets, buñuelos, tiganities, or fritters—it's all the same idea and it pops up in kitchens around the world. A piece of food, savory or sweet, is dipped into a light batter and then fried in deep, hot oil, until puffed and golden in color. Sometimes the batter and the food are mixed together and dropped by spoonfuls into the hot oil.

The entire procedure is quite simple, and once your batter is made and the oil is heated to the required temperature, everything goes very quickly. The batter can be made ahead of time, and in fact, can stay covered in the refrigerator for a couple of days. If you keep batter on hand and enough vegetable oil to fry in, you will always be prepared for making delicious, impromptu fritters to serve with cocktails or to liven up any main course.

Here are the basics you need to know about deep frying:

1. Use a deep, heavy kettle with straight sides. I have a black cast-iron fry kettle that I use just for this purpose. It should be deep enough so that the right quantity of oil (3 to 4 cups) fills it only half way. This will minimize the chances of your getting splattered by hot oil.

2. Use a deep-frying thermometer. It costs only a few dollars and

there is no other way that I know of to determine accurately when the oil is hot enough. A thermometer will also let you know when the oil temperature has dropped, so that you can increase the heat. Keep in mind that the steadier you keep the heat of the oil at the called-for temperature, the crisper the fritters will be.

3. Don't fry too many fritters at the same time—they will cool off the oil. Ideally, most fritters should be served as soon as possible after cooking. But if you need to hold them until all are cooked, keep them warm in a slow (250°) oven.

4. Get a large, long-handled skimmer to use for removing the fritters. The long handle increases the distance between you and the hot oil.

5. All the recipes call for draining the fritters on absorbent paper. This can be either paper toweling or brown paper bags saved for this purpose. I find they work equally well.

6. Although some traditional fritter recipes call for food to be fried in lard or other animal fats, I prefer to use vegetable oil. Vegetable oils can be heated to 400 degrees without burning, while animal fats burn more quickly. I find peanut or corn oil to be best, but any light vegetable oil will do. Unless you are frying shrimp or fish, you can reuse the oil a number of times. Oil used for fish can also be reused, but only for fish. When the oil has cooled, strain it through several

layers of cheesecloth, or better yet, use one of those paper coffee filters, to remove the burnt particles that can impart an unpleasant flavor to the oil. Keep the strained oil in a tightly covered jar in the refrigerator. If you have used the oil more than twice, add a little fresh oil the next time you use it.

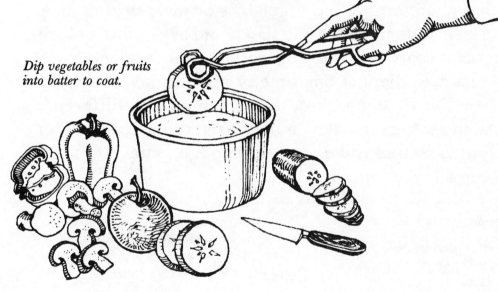

Dip vegetables or fruits into batter to coat.

A Sampler of Fritter Batters

Fritter batter can be a combination of the simplest ingredients, flour and water. Or it can include eggs, spirits of various kinds, milk, leavening, and various seasonings and spices. Its most basic quality is stickiness—it has to adhere well to vegetables or meat during deep frying. Of course, it adds crispness and flavor and a beautiful golden color to whatever it coats. All kinds of fritter batters are good, and you should try each of them at one time or another, to see for yourself how you like them and how they combine with different ingredients. All the batters can stay in the refrigerator, covered, for several days. These recipes will each yield enough batter to coat enough food for 4 to 6 people.

Fritter Batter 1—*flour and water*

This makes a very crisp, pure coating that is good to use for the very youngest, most tender vegetables.

⅔ cup all-purpose flour
 1 *cup water**

Put the flour in a small bowl. Pour in the water, mixing with a wooden spoon. Cover the bowl and let it stand at room temperature for 2 to 3 hours.

Notes and Variations

*A happy variation is to substitute 1 cup of beer (room temperature) for the water.

Fritter Batter 2—*savory beer batter*

  1 *cup all-purpose flour*
12 *ounces (1 can) beer*
1½ *teaspoons salt*
    Several grindings black pepper
  1 *tablespoon paprika*
 ¼ *teaspoon cayenne pepper*

Mix all the ingredients together with a fork or whisk in a small bowl. Cover and let stand at room temperature for 2 to 3 hours.

Fritter Batter 3—*with beaten egg whites*

The stiffly beaten egg whites folded in at the last minute provide extra lightness.

1 *cup all-purpose flour*
2 *tablespoons vegetable oil* or *melted butter*
1 *cup water*
1 *teaspoon salt*
2 *egg whites*

1. Mix the flour, oil, water, and salt together to make a thick batter. Let stand in a covered bowl at room temperature for at least 20 minutes (2 to 3 hours is better).

2. Just before you are ready to fry, beat the egg whites until they hold a peak and fold them gently into the batter.

Fritter Batter 4—*with whole eggs*

2 *eggs*
2 *tablespoons olive oil* or *vegetable oil*
¾ *cup warm water*
1 *teaspoon baking powder*
1 *teaspoon salt*
1 *cup all-purpose flour*

Beat the eggs with oil, water, baking powder, and salt. Beat in the flour. Cover and let stand 2 to 3 hours before using.

THE FRITTERS 121

Fritter Batter 5—*with brandy or whisky*

1 *cup all-purpose flour*
⅔ *cup milk*
2 *tablespoons brandy or whisky*
4 *tablespoons vegetable oil* or *melted butter*
1 *egg, separated*
1 *teaspoon salt*

1. Mix the flour, milk, brandy, oil, egg yolk, and salt together. Cover and let stand for 2 to 3 hours.

2. Just before you are ready to fry beat the egg white until stiff and fold it gently into batter.

Fritter Batter 6—*with yeast*

One of my favorites; a very light, crisp batter.

1 *package dry yeast*
¼ *cup warm water*
½ *teaspoon sugar*
1 *cup warm water*
½ *teaspoon salt*
1½ *cups all-purpose flour*

1. Sprinkle yeast and sugar into the warm water. Let stand until the yeast begins to foam, 5 to 10 minutes.

2. Add the cup of water, salt, and yeast mixture to the flour in a medium-size bowl. Beat with wooden spoon until very smooth. Cover and let rise for 1½ to 2 hours, until it has doubled in volume. Stir down and use.

Asparagus Fritters

This recipe for asparagus fritters leaves the asparagus tips very crisp and crunchy, since the tips themselves hardly cook at all. If you prefer asparagus a little more cooked, first drop the tips into boiling salted water for about 3 minutes, drain, and proceed to make the fritters.

1 *recipe Fritter Batter 4, or any other fritter batter, pages* 120–122
1 *pound asparagus tips, about 3 inches long*
3–4 *cups vegetable oil for deep frying*
   Salt
   Several grindings black pepper
   Lemon wedges

1. Prepare the fritter batter.

2. Remove any rough skin from the asparagus tips. Cut them in half so that you have pieces that are about 1½ inches long.

3. Heat the vegetable oil to 360°.

4. Dip the asparagus pieces one at a time, into the fritter batter. Drop the asparagus tips into the hot oil about 4 at a time. Fry until golden brown.

5. Remove with a slotted spoon and drain on absorbent paper. Repeat until all are done.

6. Sprinkle with salt and pepper and serve with lemon wedges.

Serves 4 to 6.

Jamaican Bean Fritters

You will be surprised at the marvelous texture of these fritters. It is well worth the time involved in preparing the peas. Serve these unusual, delicious fritters with drinks to people who enjoy spicy food.

1 *cup black-eyed peas*
2 *fresh hot red peppers, seeded and finely chopped* or 1½ *teaspoons dried red pepper flakes*
2 *teaspoons salt*
3–4 *cups vegetable oil for deep frying*

1. Soak the peas overnight in cold water.

2. In the morning, drain, and rub the peas together to rub off the skins. Continue soaking the peas. Cover with more cold water and change it frequently during the day until all the peas are skinned.

3. Drain the peas and put them, together with the salt and peppers, through a meat grinder, food processor, or electric blender.

4. Beat the mixture with a wooden spoon until it is light and fluffy and somewhat increased in bulk. Taste for seasoning and adjust if necessary. It should be quite spicy.

5. Heat the vegetable oil to 360°.

6. Drop tablespoonfuls of the mixture into the hot oil and fry until golden brown on both sides. Fry no more than 4 to 6 fritters at one time.

7. Remove with a slotted spoon and drain on absorbent paper. Repeat until all are done. Serve hot.

Yield: About 24 fritters.

Carrot Fritters

I find that carrots in any form are always a very popular vegetable with grown-ups and kids alike. These carrot fritters make a charming and tasty side dish to almost any meal and are delicious enough to serve as a snack on their own.

5–6 *carrots, grated*
  2 *eggs*
  ½ *teaspoon salt*
  1 *tablespoon sugar*
  ¼ *cup flour*
  ½ *stick butter*

1. Mix the grated carrots with eggs, salt, and sugar, and blend in the flour to make a batter the consistency of thick cream.

2. Melt the butter in a large skillet and drop batter by tablespoons into the hot butter. Fry for a few minutes on each side. Remove with a slotted spoon and drain on absorbent paper.

Yield: About 18 fritters.

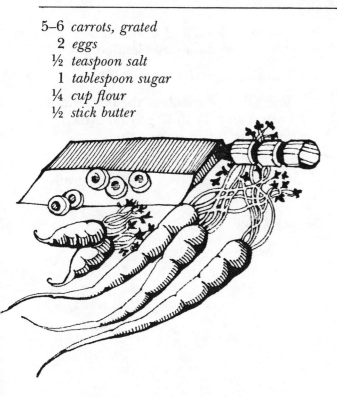

Celery Fritters

1 cup all-purpose flour
1 teaspoon baking powder
1 teaspoon salt
2 teaspoons curry powder
½ cup milk
¼ cup heavy cream
2 eggs, lightly beaten
1 bunch celery, leaves and tough parts of
    stems removed, finely chopped
3–4 cups vegetable oil for deep frying

1. Into a bowl, sift together several times the flour, baking powder, salt, and curry powder.

2. In a separate bowl, combine the milk, cream, and eggs. Mix well. Stir into the flour mixture.

3. Add the celery, and beat with a wooden spoon until well blended.

4. Heat the vegetable oil to 360°.

5. Drop tablespoonfuls of the batter into the hot oil and fry until golden brown. Fry only 4 to 6 fritters at a time.

6. Remove with a slotted spoon and drain on absorbent paper. Repeat until all are done. Serve hot.

Serves 4 to 6.

Bobs Strachan's Corn Fritters

Corn fritters are traditional with fried chicken. I like them with barbecued chicken too. In fact, I like them with almost anything and even by themselves. Mrs. Strachan says to serve them with maple syrup, and it's a good idea.

2 *cups all-purpose flour*
2 *teaspoons baking powder*
1 *teaspoon salt*
1 *egg*
½ *cup milk*
2 *cups canned cream-style corn*
1 *10-ounce package frozen kernel corn,*
    thawed
  Several grindings black pepper
3–4 *cups vegetable oil for deep frying*

1. In a medium bowl, sift together flour, baking powder, and salt.

2. Add the remaining ingredients, except for the frying oil, and mix well.

3. Heat the vegetable oil to 360°.

4. Drop tablespoonfuls of the batter into the hot oil and fry for 2 to 3 minutes, or until golden brown. Fry no more than 4 to 6 fritters at one time.

5. Remove with a slotted spoon or skimmer and drain on absorbent paper. Repeat until all are done.

Yield: About 17 fritters.

Fennel Fritters

1 *recipe any fritter batter, pages* 120–122
3–4 *fennel bulbs*
3–4 *cups vegetable oil for deep frying*
   Salt
   Several grindings black pepper
   Lemon wedges

1. Prepare the fritter batter.

2. Trim the fennel bulbs and slice into 1-inch segments.

3. Heat the vegetable oil to 360°.

4. Dip the fennel pieces into the fritter batter and drop them into the hot oil. Fry until golden brown. Fry no more than 4 to 6 fritters at one time.

5. Remove with a slotted spoon and drain on absorbent paper. Repeat until all are done.

6. To serve, sprinkle with salt and pepper and garnish with lemon wedges.

Serves 4 to 6.

Mushroom Fritters

These are unbelievably good, and like all fritters, easy to make. Serve them as hors d'oeuvres, as a first course, or for lunch with a tomato sauce.

1 *recipe any fritter batter, pages* 120–122
  (2 and 5 are especially recommended)
1 *pound mushrooms*
  Lemon juice
  Salt
3–4 *cups vegetable oil for deep frying*

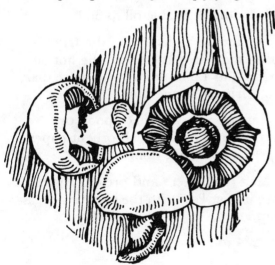

1. Prepare the fritter batter.

2. Wipe mushrooms clean. Sprinkle them with lemon juice and a little salt.

3. Heat the vegetable oil to 360°.

4. Dip the mushrooms into the fritter batter and drop them into the hot oil. Fry for 3 to 4 minutes, or until golden. Fry no more than 4 to 6 fritters at one time.

5. Remove with a slotted spoon or skimmer and drain on absorbent paper. Repeat until all are done. Serve as soon as possible, sprinkled with salt and pepper or with one of the Tomato Sauces, pages 184–186.

Serves 4 to 6.

Okra Fritters

If you like spicy foods, season the flour with quite a lot of cayenne in addition to the salt and pepper.

1 *recipe Fritter Batter 4, or any fritter batter,*
   pages 120–122
1 *pound small okra pods*
½ *cup flour*
1 *teaspoon salt*
   Several grindings black pepper
   Cayenne pepper to taste (optional)
½ *stick butter*
1 *clove garlic, put through a press*
3–4 *cups vegetable oil for deep frying*

1. Prepare the fritter batter.

2. Wash the okra pods. Remove the stems and split each pod in half.

3. Mix together the flour, salt, pepper and cayenne. Dredge the okra with the seasoned flour.

4. Heat the vegetable oil to 360°.

5. Dip the okra pieces into the fritter batter, then drop them into the hot oil. Fry for 3 to 4 minutes. Fry no more than 4 to 6 fritters at one time.

6. Remove with a slotted spoon or skimmer and drain on absorbent paper. Repeat until all are done.

7. Melt the butter* and press the garlic clove into it. Pass with the okra fritters as a dip.

Serves 4 to 6.

Notes and Variations

*Squeeze half a lemon into the garlic butter, and/or a few drops of Tabasco sauce.

Eggplant Fritters I

1 recipe Fritter Batter, 2, page 121
2 medium eggplants
　Salt
3–4 cups vegetable oil for deep frying

1. Prepare the fritter batter.

2. Peel the eggplants and cut them into 1-inch slices. Sprinkle with salt and allow to drain in a colander for at least ½ hour.

3. Pat the eggplant slices dry on a paper towel.

4. Heat the vegetable oil to 360°.

5. Dip the eggplant slices into the fritter batter. Fry in the hot oil for about 5 minutes, or until golden brown. Fry no more than 4 to 6 fritters at one time.

6. Remove with a slotted spoon and drain on absorbent paper. Repeat until all are done.

7. Serve just as they are, or with one of the Tomato Sauces on pages 184–186.

Serves 4 to 6.

Eggplant Fritters II

1½ pounds eggplant, peeled and cut into
     1-inch cubes
1 egg, lightly beaten
2 tablespoons milk
1 teaspoon salt
  Several grindings black pepper
⅛ teaspoon cayenne pepper
1 cup all-purpose flour
1 teaspoon baking powder
3–4 cups vegetable oil for deep frying
  Lemon wedges

1. Cook the eggplant in boiling salted water to cover until tender, about 15 minutes.

2. Drain the eggplant and mash it into a smooth puree.

3. Add the egg, milk, salt, pepper, and cayenne to the puree and mix well.

4. Sift together the flour and baking powder and add, by tablespoonfuls, to the eggplant mixture. Beat after each addition with a wooden spoon to mix well.

5. Heat the vegetable oil to 360°.

6. Drop tablespoonfuls of the fritter batter into the hot oil and fry for 3 to 4 minutes, or until golden brown. Fry no more than 4 to 6 fritters at one time.

7. Remove with slotted spoon and drain on absorbent paper. Repeat until all are done.

8. Serve hot, with lemon wedges.

Serves 4 to 6.

Pepper Fritters

I have made these fritters using green or red bell peppers, or a mixture of the two. The long Italian frying peppers are good also. I always make a couple of hot pepper fritters for myself and friends with fiery inclinations. These fritters make an especially nice first course when served with one of the tomato sauces on pages 184–186.

1 *recipe Fritter Batter 4, or any fritter batter, pages* 120–122
6–8 *green or red peppers*
3–4 *cups vegetable oil for deep frying*

1. Prepare the fritter batter.

2. Seed the peppers and remove the stems, and slice into ½-inch pieces.

3. Heat the vegetable oil to 360°.

4. Dip the pepper slices into the fritter batter, and drop them into the hot oil. Fry until golden brown. Fry no more than 4 to 6 fritters at one time.

5. Remove with a slotted spoon and drain on absorbent paper. Repeat until all are done. Sprinkle with salt and serve as soon as possible.

Serves 4 to 6.

Split Pea Fritters

An unusual and savory fritter from the Caribbean to serve as an accompaniment to drinks.

1 *cup split peas*
1 *medium onion*
1 *clove garlic*
1 *tablespoon curry powder (or more to taste)*
2 *teaspoons salt*
A great deal of freshly ground black pepper
3–4 *cups vegetable oil for deep frying*

1. Soak the peas overnight. The water should cover the peas by at least 3 inches. In the morning change the water, and continue soaking them until you are ready to use them.

2. Drain the peas and put through a meat grinder (fine setting), food processor, or blender, together with the onion, the garlic, and all the seasonings.

3. Beat the mixture with a wooden spoon until light and fluffy.

4. Heat the vegetable oil to 360°.

5. Drop tablespoonfuls of the fritter mixture into the hot oil and fry until golden brown. Fry no more than 4 to 6 fritters at one time.

6. Remove with a slotted spoon and drain on absorbent paper. Repeat until all are done. Serve hot.

Yield: About 24 fritters; serves 4 to 6.

Cheese Fritters

Serve these instead of potatoes with a roast beef, or any other roast.

1 *cup beer* or *water*
¾ *stick butter, cut into small pieces*
1 *teaspoon salt*
1 *cup all-purpose flour*
4 *eggs*
4 *ounces grated Gruyère cheese* or *any other hard cheese*
  Several grindings black pepper
¼ *teaspoon cayenne pepper*
3–4 *cups vegetable oil for deep frying*

1. Put the beer, butter, and salt into a medium saucepan. Boil gently until the butter has melted.

2. Pour the flour all at once into the saucepan and beat with a wooden spoon until the mixture forms a mass and leaves the sides of the pan. Remove from heat.

3. Beat in the eggs, one at a time, beating until each is completely blended into the batter. (If you have a food processor, transfer the batter to the food processor bowl and beat in the eggs, one by one, using the steel blade.)

4. Add the grated cheese, pepper, and cayenne. Beat until well blended.

5. Heat the vegetable oil to 360°.

6. Drop teaspoonfuls of the fritter batter into the vegetable oil. Do only a few at a time as they will puff up. Fry until golden brown.

7. Remove with a slotted spoon and drain on absorbent paper. Repeat until all are done. Serve warm.

Serves 4 to 6.

Curried Oyster Fritters

2 cups all-purpose flour
2 teaspoons baking powder
2 teaspoons salt
2 teaspoons curry powder
⅛ teaspoon cayenne pepper
  Several grindings black pepper
2 eggs, lightly beaten
½ cup milk
½ cup oyster liquid
1 cup drained fresh or frozen oysters
3–4 cups vegetable oil for deep frying

1. Into a medium bowl, sift together the flour and baking powder. Add the salt, curry powder, cayenne, and black pepper.

2. In a separate bowl, combine the eggs, milk, and oyster liquid. Add this mixture to the flour and mix well to form a batter.

3. Chop the oysters coarsely and blend into the batter.

4. Heat the vegetable oil to 360°.

5. Drop tablespoonfuls of the fritter batter into the hot oil and fry for about 3 minutes, or until golden brown. Fry no more than 4 to 6 fritters at one time.

6. Remove with a slotted spoon and drain on absorbent paper. Repeat until all are done. Serve hot.

Yield: About 35 fritters.

Oyster Fritters II

These fritters are delicious served with Remoulade Sauce, page 187.

1 *recipe any fritter batter, pages*
    120–122 (I like 2)
24 *oysters, shucked*
   Juice of 1 lemon
   Salt
   Flour for dredging
3–4 *cups vegetable oil for deep frying*

1. Prepare the fritter batter.

2. Drain the oysters and sprinkle them with the lemon juice and salt.

3. Heat the vegetable oil to 360°.

4. Dredge the oysters with flour. Dip each oyster into the fritter batter, then drop into the hot oil. Fry until golden brown. Fry no more than 4 to 6 fritters at one time.

5. Remove with a slotted spoon and drain on absorbent paper. Repeat until all are done.

Serves 4 to 6.

Drop fritters into hot oil.

Vietnamese Shrimp Fritters

Serve these fritters alone, or try one of the Vinegar-Soy sauces, page 178, as a dipping sauce to pass around with the fritters.

1½ cups all-purpose flour
1 teaspoon baking powder
3 eggs, lightly beaten
1 cup water
1 pound small shrimp, shelled, deveined, and sliced in half, lengthwise
4 scallions, coarsely chopped
2 carrots, coarsely chopped
1 celery stalk, coarsely chopped
1 clove garlic, put through a garlic press
2 teaspoons salt
1½ teaspoons ground coriander
⅛ teaspoon cayenne pepper
Several grindings black pepper
3–4 cups vegetable oil for deep frying

1. In a medium bowl, mix together the flour, baking powder, eggs, and water. Add the remaining ingredients, except for the vegetable oil, and mix well.

2. Heat the vegetable oil to 360°.

3. Drop soupspoonfuls of the fritter batter into the hot oil and fry for about 4 minutes, or until fritters are golden brown on both sides. Fry no more than 4 to 6 fritters at one time.

4. Remove with a slotted spoon and drain on absorbent paper. Repeat until all are done. Serve hot.

Yield: About 24 fritters; serves 4 to 6.

Marinated Shrimp Fritters

Marinade

6 *tablespoons olive oil*
2 *tablespoons lemon juice*
1 *teaspoon fresh or dried tarragon*
   A few drops of Tabasco Sauce
1 *teaspoon salt*
   Several grindings black pepper

12 *jumbo shrimps, shelled and deveined*
1 *recipe Fritter Batter 3, page 121*
   Flour for sprinkling
3–4 *cups vegetable oil for deep frying*

1. Mix together the marinade ingredients. Marinate the shrimp overnight.

2. Prepare the fritter batter.

3. Drain the shrimp and pat dry. Sprinkle them with flour.

4. Heat the vegetable oil to 360°.

5. Dip shrimp one at a time into the fritter batter, then drop into the hot oil. Fry until golden brown. Fry no more than 4 to 6 shrimp at one time.

6. Remove with slotted spoon and drain on absorbent paper. Repeat until all are done.

7. Serve the shrimps hot either with Remoulade Sauce, page 187, or accompanied by lemon wedges.

Serves 4 to 6.

Oyster Balls

1½ cups oysters, shucked, drained, and finely
    chopped (reserve the oyster liquid)
¼ cup reserved oyster liquid
4 tablespoons all-purpose flour
⅛ teaspoon baking soda
4 eggs, lightly beaten
6 scallions, finely chopped (green tops
    included)
1 teaspoon grated fresh ginger root
½ teaspoon salt
⅛ teaspoon monosodium glutamate
    (optional)
  Several grindings black pepper
3–4 cups peanut or vegetable oil for deep
    frying

1. In a medium bowl, combine the oysters, oyster liquid, flour, baking soda, eggs, scallions, and all the seasonings. Mix well.

2. Heat the peanut or vegetable oil to 360°.

3. Drop spoonfuls of the fritter batter into the hot oil and fry until golden brown. Fry no more than 4 to 6 fritters at one time.

4. Remove with a slotted spoon and drain on absorbent paper. Repeat until all are done.

5. Serve* with one of the Vinegar-Soy Sauces, page 178.

Serves 4 to 6.

Notes and Variations

*Although these oyster balls are best when served immediately, they can be kept warm in a slow (250°) oven for half an hour or so.

Shrimp Balls

Delicate and delicious, shrimp balls are nice with drinks or as part of a larger dumpling assortment. Once you have shelled and deveined the shrimp, the shrimp balls are made in minutes.

1 *pound raw shrimp, shelled, deveined, and washed*
1½ *ounces fresh pork fat*
1½ *slices white bread, diced and sprinkled with 2 tablespoons chicken stock or water*
1 *egg, separated*
4 *water chestnuts, finely chopped*
½ *teaspoon grated fresh ginger root*
1 *teaspoon salt*
Several grindings black pepper
3–4 *cups peanut or vegetable oil for deep frying*

1. Chop together the shrimp and pork fat to make a smooth paste. Use a food processor, blender, meat grinder, or food mill.

2. In a medium bowl, combine the shrimp mixture with the bread, egg yolk, water chestnuts, ginger root, salt, and pepper. Mix well.

3. Heat the peanut or vegetable oil to 360°.

4. Beat the egg white until stiff and fold into the shrimp mixture.

5. Drop soupspoonfuls of the shrimp mixture into the hot oil and fry about 3 minutes, or until golden brown. Fry no more than 4 to 6 fritters at one time.

6. Remove with a slotted spoon and drain on absorbent paper. Repeat until all are done. Keep warm in a slow (250°) oven until they are all done.

7. Serve with one of Vinegar-Soy Sauces, page 178.

Yield: About 18 shrimp balls.

Ham and Almond Fritters

Drop these fritters from a teaspoon into the hot fat and you will have perfect small hors d'oeuvres. Use a tablespoon to drop the batter and the fritters will be larger: perfect as a light main course.

1	*cup water*
1	*stick butter*
1	*cup all–purpose flour*
4	*eggs*
½	*cup grated Gruyère*
½	*cup cooked lean ham cut into very small pieces*
¼	*cup slivered blanched almonds*
	Salt and pepper to taste
3–4	*cups vegetable oil for deep frying*

1. Combine the water and butter in a saucepan and bring to a boil. Remove from heat and add flour all at once. Beat with a wooden spoon until the mixture leaves the sides of the pan.

2. Beat in the eggs, one at a time, completely blending each egg before adding the next.

3. Stir in the cheese, ham, almonds, and salt and pepper to taste. Let stand for 15 minutes.

4. Heat the oil to 360°.

5. Drop the batter by spoonfuls into the hot oil and fry until the fritters are golden brown. Remove and drain on absorbent paper.

Yield: About 20 hors d'oeuvre-size fritters.

Chicken Liver Fritters

½ *pound chicken livers*
¼ *cup port or Madeira*
1 *recipe any fritter batter, pages* 120–122
Salt
Several grindings black pepper
Flour for dredging
3–4 *cups vegetable oil for deep frying*
Lemon juice

1. Cut the raw chicken livers into bite-sized pieces and marinate in the port or Madeira for about 2 hours.

2. Prepare the fritter batter.

3. Drain the chicken livers. Sprinkle them with salt and pepper and dredge in flour.

4. Heat the vegetable oil to 360°.

5. Dip each liver piece into the fritter batter and drop it into the hot oil. Fry until golden. Fry no more than 4 to 6 fritters at one time.

6. Remove with a slotted spoon and drain on absorbent paper. Repeat until all are done.

7. Serve sprinkled with lemon juice.

Serves 6 as an hors d'oeuvre.

Peanut Butter Fritters

An unusual snack from the Orient. Try passing a plate of these around next time friends have the munchies.

½ cup brown sugar
⅔ cup water
1½ cups rice flour
1 cup crunchy peanut butter
½ cup sesame seeds
3–4 cups vegetable oil for deep drying

1. In a medium saucepan, dissolve the sugar in the water over medium heat. Bring to a boil. Remove from heat and stir in the rice flour to form a dough.

2. Knead the dough for 1 minute or so, then pinch off enough dough to make balls the size of Ping-Pong balls.

3. Flatten each ball with the palm of your hand. Place a teaspoon of peanut butter in the center of each. Seal the edges and form into a ball again between your palms. Then roll in sesame seeds to cover.

4. Heat the vegetable oil to 360°.

5. Drop the fritter balls into the hot oil and fry until golden. Fry no more than 4 to 6 fritters at one time.

6. Remove with a slotted spoon and drain on absorbent paper. Repeat until all are done. Serve.

Serves 4 to 6.

Tempura

Tempura, that most elegant of fritter dishes from Japan, turns out not to be Japanese at all, but rather Portugese in origin, said to have been introduced to Japan by missionaries sometime in the late 1500s.

Batter

 3 *egg yolks*
 2 *cups cold water*
2½ *cups flour*

Foods for Coating*

Shrimp, raw, shelled except for the very tip of the tail, and deveined. Make shallow crosswise cuts with a sharp knife on the underside of each shrimp in 3 places.
Fish fillets, cut into small pieces
Mushrooms
String beans, ends snipped off
Carrots, julienned
Sweet potatoes, sliced
Eggplant, peeled and sliced
Onions, sliced in rings
Zucchini, sliced

3–4 *cups vegetable oil for deep frying*

Tempura Sauce, page 181

1. Mix the egg yolks and water. Use chopsticks to stir in the flour. Stir very little, leaving the batter lumpy.

2. Prepare all foods for coating.

3. Heat the vegetable oil to 360°.

4. Dip each item into the batter and fry in oil for 1 to 3 minutes, until golden.

5. Remove with chopsticks or a slotted spoon, drain on absorbent paper, and serve. Each person should have a small bowl of Tempura Sauce at his or her place.

Notes and Variations

* You may choose all or any combination of foods for coating, depending on what you feel like eating and how many people you are serving. Sometimes I omit the shrimp and fish, making an all-vegetable tempura. Very economical and quite delicious.

The Sweet Dumplings

Notes on Sweet Dumplings

The sweet dumplings in this section are comprised essentially of filled dumplings and fritters. While on the face of it sweet dumplings may appear to be the same as dessert dumplings, this is not necessarily the case. Some of these dumplings make quite a meal in themselves: Calas, the New Orleans rice fritters, and buñuelos are traditionally eaten for breakfast; cheese-filled vareniki are prime candidates for breakfast or lunch dishes. Many others, of course, do make wonderful dessert dishes—proof, if proof is necessary, that there is a place for dumplings in every part of the menu.

Apple Fritters I

Apple fritters of one sort or another pop up in cuisines the world over. Almost any way you make them, they are delicious. Serve them for dessert, a snack, or even for breakfast.

1 *recipe Fritter Batter 1,* page* 120
  (using beer instead of water)
¼ *cup sugar*
  Grated rind of 1 lemon
3 *tablespoons rum or kirsch*
3 *apples, peeled, cored, and sliced*
3–4 *cups vegetable oil for deep frying*
  Confectioner's sugar

1. Prepare the fritter batter.

2. In a medium bowl, mix together the ¼ cup sugar, lemon rind, and rum or kirsch. Marinate the apple slices in this mixture for 1 hour.

3. Remove the apple slices and pat dry.

4. Heat the vegetable oil to 360°.

5. Dip the apple slices into the fritter batter and drop them into the hot oil. Fry for about 3 minutes, or until golden brown on each side. Fry no more than 4 to 6 fritters at one time.

6. Remove with a slotted spoon and drain on absorbent paper. Repeat until all are done.

7. Sprinkle with confectioner's sugar and serve.

Serves 4 to 6.

Notes and Variations

*For a completely different kind of apple fritter, try Fritter Batter 6 (with yeast) on page 122.

Apple Fritters II

1½ cups all-purpose flour
2 tablespoons sugar
½ teaspoon baking soda
¼ teaspoon salt
½ teaspoon mace
½ teaspoon cinnamon
1 egg
¾ cup buttermilk
3 large apples, peeled, cored, and coarsely
   chopped
3–4 cups vegetable oil for deep frying
   Confectioner's sugar

1. Into a medium bowl, sift together the flour, sugar, baking soda, salt, mace, and cinnamon. Add the egg and milk. Mix well.

2. Stir in the chopped apples.

3. Heat the vegetable oil to 360°.

4. Drop soupspoonfuls of the fritter batter into the hot oil and fry for about 4 minutes, or until golden. Fry no more than 4 to 6 fritters at one time.

5. Remove with a slotted spoon and drain on absorbent paper. Repeat until all are done.

6. Sprinkle with confectioner's sugar and serve.

Serves 4 to 6.

Blackberry Dumplings

These dumplings can be made with strawberries, raspberries, blueberries, or other berries in season.

1½ *cups flour*
  1 *teaspoon salt*
  1 *stick cold butter*
  2 *tablespoons lard or solid white shortening*
⅓ *cup ice water*
  1 *pint blackberries, picked over and washed*
⅓ *cup sugar*
1½ *teaspoons flour*
    Lemon juice for sprinkling over berries
  2 *tablespoons butter*

1. In a medium bowl, mix together the 1½ cups flour and salt. Cut in the stick of cold butter and shortening to form a mixture that is the consistency of coarse oatmeal. Add water to make a dough and form into a ball. Cover and refrigerate for at least 2 hours.

2. In a separate bowl, mix the blackberries with the sugar and 1½ teaspoons flour. Sprinkle with lemon juice.

3. Roll out the dough on a floured board, and cut it into six 4-inch squares. Place 1 to 2 tablespoons of blackberries on each square and dot with butter. Fold each square over to form a triangle. Moisten the edges with a little water, if necessary, and press down on the edges with the tines of a fork.

4. Preheat the oven to 375°.

5. Arrange the dumplings on a buttered baking sheet, and bake for 25 minutes, or until they are golden.

6. Serve warm just as they are or with sweetened whipped cream.

Serves 4 to 6.

Banana-Rum Fritters

6 *firm, but ripe, bananas*
½ *cup rum*
½ *cup orange juice*
3 *tablespoons all-purpose flour*
3 *tablespoons cornstarch*
3 *egg whites*
3 *tablespoons butter*
½ *cup sugar*
3–4 *cups vegetable oil for deep frying*

1. Slice the bananas into 1-inch lengths, and marinate in a bowl with the rum and orange juice for ½ hour.

2. In a medium bowl, mix together the flour, cornstarch, and egg whites to form a batter.

3. Drain the bananas (reserving the liquid) and pat them dry on paper towels.

4. Put the rum and orange juice, butter, and sugar into a saucepan. Simmer for 20 minutes, or longer, to melt the butter and reduce the liquid by ⅓.

5. Heat the vegetable oil to 360°.

6. Dip the banana pieces into the batter, and drop them into the hot oil. Fry for 3 minutes, or until golden brown. Fry no more than 4 to 6 fritters at one time.

7. Remove with a slotted spoon, and drain on absorbent paper. Repeat until all are done.

8. Place the bananas in a buttered serving dish. Pour the syrup over them to serve. They may be reheated in a slow (250°) oven, if necessary.

Serves 6 to 8.

Buñuelos from Mexico

These deep-fried puffs of batter, sprinkled with cinnamon and sugar, are delicious anytime, but great for breakfast.

4 *cups all-purpose flour*
1 *tablespoon sugar*
1 *teaspoon baking powder*
1 *teaspoon salt*
2 *eggs*
1 *cup milk*
½ *stick butter, melted*
3–4 *cups vegetable oil for deep frying*

To serve

*Additional sugar and cinnamon.**

1. Into a medium bowl, sift together the flour, sugar, baking powder, and salt.

2. Add the eggs, milk, and melted butter. Mix to form a soft dough.

3. Remove the dough to a floured board, and knead until it feels smooth and satiny.

4. Divide dough into walnut-size pieces. Cover with a cloth and let stand for ½ hour.

5. Heat the vegetable oil to 360°.

6. Flatten each ball into a flat pancake between the palms of your hands and drop into the hot oil about 4 at a time. Fry for 4 to 5 minutes, or until puffed and brown.

7. Remove with a slotted spoon and drain on absorbent paper. Repeat until all are done.

8. Sprinkle with sugar and cinnamon and serve.

Yield: About 4 dozen buñuelos.

Notes and Variations

*Another popular way to serve buñuelos is with a sweet Anise Syrup, page 188.

Pineapple Fritters

1 *recipe Fritter Batter* 5, *page* 122
4 *tablespoons sugar*
1 *medium-size fresh pineapple*
¼ *cup rum or cognac*
3–4 *cups vegetable oil for deep frying*

1. Prepare Fritter Batter 5, adding 2 tablespoons of the sugar to it.

2. Peel the pineapple and cut it into slices about ¾ inch thick. Cut the slices into quarters.

3. Combine 2 tablespoons sugar and rum or cognoc and let the pineapple slices marinate in this for 1 hour.

4. Heat the oil to 360°.

5. Drain the pineapple slices, dip them a few at a time into the batter, and then drop them into hot oil. Fry until golden brown. Remove with a slotted spoon and drain on absorbent paper. Repeat until all are done.

6. Serve sprinkled with sugar or Pineapple-Rum Sauce, page 189 or Lemon Sauce, page 186.

Serves 6 to 8.

Samsa
fried sweet walnut dumplings from central Asia

Dough

1½ cups all-purpose flour
⅔ cup warm water
½ teaspoon salt
4 tablespoons butter, softened to room
    temperature

Filling

6 ounces shelled walnuts, pulverized in
    blender or food processor
¼ stick butter, softened to room temperature
1½ tablespoons sugar
3–4 cups vegetable oil for deep frying
    Confectioner's sugar

1. In a medium bowl, mix together the flour, water, salt, and 2 tablespoons of the butter. Beat with a wooden spoon to make a firm dough. Gather the dough into a ball. Cover and let rest for 30 minutes.

2. In another bowl, mix together the ingredients for the filling.

3. Roll the dough into a rectangle approximately 16 by 18 inches and smear the remaining 2 tablespoons of butter over the dough. Fold the rectangle into quarters and roll it out again as thin as possible. Cut into 2-inch squares.

4. Place about a teaspoon of filling in the center of each square and bring the 4 corners up to meet in the middle. Pinch the edges and corners together to seal completely. Moisten your fingers with water if necessary.

5. Heat the vegetable oil to 360°.

6. Drop about 6 samsa at a time into the hot oil, and fry for 3 minutes or until golden brown.

7. Remove with a slotted spoon and drain on absorbent paper. Repeat until all are done.

8. Sprinkle with confectioner's sugar and serve.

Serves 6 to 8.

Rum Cherry Fritters

½ cup all-purpose flour
2 eggs, separated
2 tablespoons confectioner's sugar
2 tablespoons rum
¼ teaspoon salt
½ cup clarified butter
½ cup vegetable oil
1 pound cherries with stems
  Confectioner's sugar

1. In a medium bowl, mix together the flour, egg yolks, 2 tablespoons confectioner's sugar, rum, and salt to form a smooth batter. Cover and let stand 1 to 2 hours.

2. Beat the egg whites until they are stiff and fold them into the batter.

3. Heat the butter and vegetable oil in a large frying pan to 360°, then turn the heat to low.

4. Dip the cherries into the batter and stand them up in the hot oil. Fry for 3 minutes, or until they are golden brown.

5. Remove the cherries. Dip them into the confectioner's sugar and serve.

Serves 6 to 8.

Notes and Variations

Another way to prepare cherry fritters is to tie together the stems of 5 cherries to form a bunch. Dip the bunch of cherries into the batter and deep fry in 3 to 4 cups of hot (360°) vegetable oil.

Lemon Fritters

2 cups all-purpose flour
1 egg
1 cup milk
1 tablespoon sugar
¼ teaspoon salt
2 tablespoons lemon juice
  Grated rind of 1 lemon
3–4 cups vegetable oil for deep frying
  Confectioner's sugar

1. In a medium bowl, combine the flour, egg, milk, sugar, salt, and lemon juice. Mix well to form a batter. Add the lemon rind and mix well.

2. Cover and let stand for 1 to 2 hours.

3. Heat the vegetable oil to 360°.

4. Drop spoonfuls of the batter into the hot oil and fry for 3 to 4 minutes, or until golden brown. Do not fry more than 4 to 6 fritters at one time.

5. Remove with a slotted spoon and drain on absorbent paper.

6. Repeat until all are done. Sprinkle with confectioner's sugar and serve, hot or cold.

Serves 4 to 6.

Notes and Variations

Dress up these lemon fritters with either the Lemon Sauce, page 186 or the Raspberry Sauce, page 190.

Orange Puffs

Crispy, orange-flavored fritters from Colombia, South America.

2 cups all-purpose flour
2 tablespoons sugar
½ teaspoon salt
2 tablespoons butter
1 cup freshly squeezed orange juice
1 tablespoon grated orange peel
3–4 cups vegetable oil for deep frying
   Confectioner's sugar

1. In a medium bowl, sift together the flour, sugar, and salt. Add the butter, orange juice, and orange peel and mix to form a stiff dough.

2. Remove the dough to a floured board and knead for about 10 minutes, or until the dough feels smooth and satiny. Cover and let stand ½ hour.

3. Roll out the dough as thin as possible. Use one or several cookie cutters to cut out shapes you like.

4. Heat the vegetable oil to 360°.

5. Drop the dough pieces into the hot oil and fry for 3 minutes, or until puffy and golden brown. Fry no more than 4 to 6 fritters at one time.

6. Remove with a slotted spoon and drain on absorbent paper. Repeat until all are done.

7. Sprinkle with confectioner's sugar and serve.

Serves 4 to 6.

Plum Dumplings

Served with sour cream, these dumplings make a very nice and unusual late Sunday breakfast.

3 cups all-purpose flour
1 teaspoon salt
2 eggs, lightly beaten
½ stick butter, softened to room temperature
½–¾ cup milk
¼ cup sugar
1 teaspoon cinnamon
⅛ teaspoon nutmeg
16 blue (Italian) plums*, pitted and sprinkled with lemon juice
7–8 quarts salted water

Topping:

½ cup ground walnuts or ½ cup breadcrumbs, fried for a few minutes in ½ stick butter

1. Sift together the flour and salt into a medium bowl.

2. Beat the eggs into the softened butter until they are well blended. Then stir into the flour, adding just enough milk to form a stiff dough.

3. Remove the dough to a well-floured board and knead for about 10 minutes, or until it feels smooth and satiny. Roll the dough into a ball. Cover and let rest for 30 minutes.

4. Into a small bowl, combine the sugar, cinnamon, and nutmeg, and mix.

5. Divide the dough in half, and roll each section out to a thickness of about ⅛ inch. Use a 3-inch round cookie cutter to cut out rounds.

6. Place a plum (2 halves) in the center of each round. Sprinkle with the sugar mixture and cover with another round of dough. Seal the edges firmly by pressing down all around with the tines of a fork.

7. Bring the salted water to a boil, and drop in 8 to 10 dumplings. Simmer for 12 minutes.

8. Remove with a slotted spoon and place them in a well-buttered ovenproof dish. Repeat until all are done.

9. Top with buttered walnuts or breadcrumbs and sprinkle with any remaining cinnamon sugar. Serve while they are still warm.

Yield: About 16 dumplings.

Notes and Variations

*1. Instead of plums, use apricots, cherries, or peaches.

2. Hungarians substitute 1½ cups of mashed potatoes for ½ the flour.

Peach Fritters

12 *peaches*
Juice from ½ lemon
2 *cups all-purpose flour*
2 *cups white dessert wine*
4 *eggs, separated*
¼ *teaspoon salt*
1 *tablespoon vegetable oil*
3–4 *cups vegetable oil for deep drying*
Confectioner's sugar

1. To peel the peaches, drop them into a pot of boiling water for 1 minute. Remove, and as soon as you can handle them, peel off the skin. Cut each peach in half and remove the pit. Sprinkle the peach halves with lemon juice to keep them from discoloring.

2. In a medium bowl, mix together the flour, white wine, egg yolks, salt, and 1 tablespoon of vegetable oil to form a batter. Let stand for 1 to 2 hours.

3. Beat the egg whites until stiff and fold them into the batter.

4. Heat the vegetable oil to 360°.

5. Dip each peach half into the batter, and drop into the hot oil. Fry for about 3 minutes, or until it is golden brown. Fry no more than 4 to 6 fritters at one time.

6. Remove with a slotted spoon and drain on absorbent paper. Repeat until all are done.

7. Sprinkle with confectioner's sugar and serve.

Yield: 24 peach fritters; serves 4 to 6.

Soufflé Fritters

The eggs will make these fritters puff up like a soufflé when they are immersed in the hot oil.

1 *cup water*
1 *stick butter*
¼ *teaspoon salt*
2 *cups all-purpose flour*
6 *eggs*
  Black currant jam or *your favorite jam*
3–4 *cups vegetable oil for deep frying*
  Confectioner's sugar

1. Place the water, butter, and salt in a medium saucepan and boil gently until the butter is melted. Remove from heat and add the flour, all at once, stirring vigorously with a wooden spoon. Put the pan back over a low flame and keep stirring until the mixture forms a ball and leaves the sides of the saucepan.

2. Off the heat, beat in the eggs, one at a time, blending each egg thoroughly before adding the next one.

3. Refrigerate the dough for 2 hours.

4. Divide the dough in half and roll out into 2 sausages. Pinch off dough to make walnut-size balls. Flatten each ball between the palms of your hands and put a teaspoon of jam in the center. Roll back into a ball.

5. Heat the vegetable oil to 360°.

6. Drop the balls into the hot oil no more than 4 at a time. Fry until golden brown.

7. Remove with a slotted spoon and drain on absorbent paper. Repeat until all are done.

8. Sprinkle with confectioner's sugar and serve.

Serves 6 to 8.

Zucchini Flower Fritters

If you have a garden and plant zucchini, you will be well supplied with these pretty golden flowers. These fritters are very popular in Eastern Europe and Italy. They make a lovely and unusual dessert. Acacia or elderberry flowers may be substituted for the zucchini flowers.

2 *cups flour*
2 *cups white dessert wine*
4 *eggs, separated*
¼ *teaspoon salt*
1 *tablespoon vegetable oil*
2 *dozen squash flowers*
3–4 *cups vegetable oil for deep frying*
Confectioner's sugar

1. Into a medium bowl, mix together the flour, wine, egg yolks, salt, and 1 tablespoon oil to form a batter. Cover and let stand 1 to 2 hours.

2. Whip the egg whites until they are stiff and fold them into the batter.

3. Heat the vegetable oil to 360°.

4. Dip the squash flowers into the batter, and drop into the hot oil. Fry for about 2 minutes, or until golden brown. Fry no more than 4 fritters at one time.

5. Remove with a slotted spoon and drain on absorbent paper. Repeat until all are done.

6. Sprinkle with confectioner's sugar and serve.

Serves 4 to 6.

Bulgarian Yogurt Fritters

1 cup unflavored yogurt
½ teaspoon baking soda
½ cup water
2 eggs, well beaten
4 cups all-purpose flour
½ teaspoon salt
3–4 cups vegetable oil for deep frying
   Confectioner's sugar
   Raspberry Sauce, page 190

1. In a medium bowl, mix together the yogurt with the baking soda, water, and eggs. Add the flour and salt. Mix well and beat with a wooden spoon until there are bubbles in the dough. Cover and let stand for 30 minutes.

2. Heat the vegetable oil to 360°.

3. Pull off walnut-size pieces of dough, roll into balls, and flatten between the palms of your hands.

4. Drop the dough rounds into the hot oil about 4 at a time. Fry until golden brown on both sides.

5. Remove with a slotted spoon and drain on absorbent paper. Repeat until all are done.

6. Sprinkle with confectioner's sugar and serve with Raspberry Sauce.

Yield: About 20 fritters.

Calas yeasted rice fritters from New Orleans

"Bel calas, bel calas tout chauds!" was the cry heard in the streets of the French Quarter at breakfast time, as Creole women carried wooden bowls of hot calas on their heads, selling them to eat with the morning cup of thick New Orleans coffee. Now you have to put them up the night before to have them for Sunday breakfast. Served with some good sausage and an assortment of honey, syrups, and jams, calas make an unusual and delicious breakfast.

½ cup rice
3 cups water
1 tablespoon butter
1 teaspoon salt
1 package dry yeast
½ cup warm water
  Pinch of sugar
3 eggs, lightly beaten
1 cup all-purpose flour
½ cup sugar
¼ teaspoon vanilla
¼ teaspoon nutmeg
3–4 cups vegetable oil for deep frying

1. Cook the rice in the water with butter and salt for 45 minutes, or until very soft

2. Drain the rice, and mash it with a potato masher or a wooden spoon. Allow to cool until it is lukewarm.

3. Dissolve the yeast in the warm water with the pinch of sugar. Let stand until the yeast begins to foam, about 5 minutes. Add this to the rice and beat well, with a wooden spoon, for at least 2 minutes. Cover, and set in a warm place to rise for at least 2 hours, or even better, overnight.

4. Add the eggs, flour, sugar, vanilla, and nutmeg. Mix well. Cover the bowl and put it in a warm place to rise for 30 minutes.

5. Heat the vegetable oil to 360°.

6. Drop tablespoonfuls of the batter into the hot oil, a few at a time. Fry until the calas are a golden color.

7. Remove with a slotted spoon and drain on absorbent paper. Keep them warm in a slow (250°) oven until all are done.

Yield: About 30 calas.

Notes and Variations

1. Calas can be reheated in the oven (350°) for about 20 minutes, but they are so good cold, mine never last long enough to make it back into the oven.

2. Try them with a good homemade applesauce.

A bowl of calas.

Oliebollen   sweet fried dumplings from Holland

¼ cup warm water
¼ cup sugar, plus ¼ teaspoon sugar
1 package active dry yeast
2 cups all-purpose flour
2 cups lukewarm milk
⅓ cup raisins
1 apple, peeled, cored, and chopped
¼ cup candied lemon peel (or orange peel), chopped
Juice of ½ lemon
Pinch salt
3–4 cups vegetable oil for deep frying
Confectioner's sugar

1. Place the warm water into a small bowl together with ¼ teaspoon of the sugar. Dissolve the yeast in warm water and let it proof.

2. Combine the flour with the remaining ¼ cup sugar, milk, and yeast mixture to make a soft dough. Cover the bowl and let stand in a warm place for 1½ to 2 hours until the dough has doubled in bulk.

3. Stir down the dough and stir in the raisins, apple, lemon peel, lemon juice, and salt. Stir well to blend.

4. Heat the oil to 360°.

5. Drop tablespoonfuls of the dough into the hot oil, a few at a time, and fry the dumplings until they are golden brown on all sides. You will need to turn them several times. Remove with a slotted spoon and drain on absorbent paper.

6. Sprinkle with confectioner's sugar and serve hot or cold.

Yield: About 30 dumplings.

Sweet Vareniki

Sweet vareniki, Ukrainian dumplings, can be filled with either cheese or fruit and served with a great deal of melted butter and sour cream They are not really a dessert, but more a meal in themselves. I like to make a meal of them in the middle of the day. Try them on a summer Sunday. Here is a choice of two vareniki doughs and three fillings.

Dough 1—with buckwheat flour*

The addition of buckwheat flour makes an unusual and delicious dumpling dough.

1½ cups all-purpose flour
1 cup buckwheat flour
1 teaspoon salt
3 egg yolks
   Approximately ¾ cup milk

1. Into a medium bowl, sift together the 2 flours with the salt. Add the egg yolks and enough milk to form a stiff dough.

2. Remove the dough to a floured board, and knead until the dough feels smooth and satiny (about 10 minutes).

3. Roll into a ball, cover, and let rest for 30 minutes, or until you are ready to use.

*You can purchase buckwheat flour in health food stores.

Dough 2—with white flour only

2 cups all-purpose flour
1 teaspoon salt
1 egg
½ cup milk

Make the dough as directed for Dough 1.

Filling 1—with cheese

1 *pound dry cottage cheese, farmer cheese, or pot cheese*
1 *stick butter, softened to room temperature*
1 *egg*
2 *tablespoons sugar*

1. Press the cheese through a sieve into a bowl.

2. Beat in the softened butter with a wooden spoon until well blended.

3. Beat in the egg and the sugar. Refrigerate for at least 1 hour before using.

Filling 2—with cherries

If you can find sour cherries, they are the best to use.

1½ *pounds sour cherries* or *Bing cherries*
½ *cup sugar*
Juice of ½ lemon for Bing cherries

1. Pit the cherries and place them in a large enameled or stainless steel saucepan. Reserve 6 cherry pits. Pour sugar over the cherries and mix. If you are not using sour cherries, use a little less sugar and add the lemon juice.

2. Let the cherries stand, in the sun if possible, for 3 hours.

3. Crack the 6 cherry pits and add them to the cherries. Place the saucepan over moderate heat and bring to a boil. Cover and lower heat. Simmer for 5 minutes.

4. Drain the cherries and reserve the juice. Discard the pits. Put this juice back into the pan and boil uncovered for 2 minutes, to reduce. Reserve for serving.

Filling 3—with blueberries

1 *pint blueberries*
5 *tablespoons sugar*

Place the blueberries in a bowl, sprinkle with sugar, and mix well. Let stand until ready to use.

To Make the Vareniki

2 *egg whites*
7–8 *quarts salted water*

1. Divide the dough of your choice in half or thirds.

2. Roll out the dough on a well-floured board until it is as thin as a dime.

3. Use a 3-inch round cookie cutter to cut out rounds.

4. Whip the egg whites until frothy and paint each round with a film of egg white.

5. Place a teaspoon of one of the fillings on each round. Bring 2 sides together to form a half moon. Pinch the edges firmly closed.

6. Bring the salted water to a boil and drop in the vareniki, about 10 at a time. Simmer for 5 to 6 minutes, or until they float to the top.

7. Remove with a slotted spoon to a well-buttered ovenproof dish. Pour a little melted butter over the vareniki and keep them warm in a slow (250°) oven until they are all done and you are ready to serve.

8. Serve with additional melted butter, sour cream, and fruit syrup.

Serves 4 to 6.

Apple Dumplings

The idea of a whole apple encased in flaky pastry seems to be universally appealing and many countries have a version of this popular dessert. They are easy to make and fun to serve.

Dough

2 cups all-purpose flour
1 teaspoon salt
1 stick unsalted butter
4 tablespoons lard
⅓–½ cup ice water

Filling

6 apples, peeled and cored and sprinkled
   with lemon juice to keep from
   discoloring
½ cup raisins soaked in rum for ½ hour
1½ cups brown sugar
¾ cup water
2 tablespoons butter

1. Mix the flour and salt together into a bowl. Cut the butter and lard into the flour using 2 knives, a pastry blender, or your fingers, until the mixture resembles a coarse meal. Add enough ice water to make a dough that holds together, and form into a ball. Cover and refrigerate for 1 to 2 hours.

2. Roll the dough out to a thickness of ¼ inch and cut it into 6 squares.

3. Place an apple in each square and fill the cavity with a tablespoon or so of rum-soaked raisins. Top the raisins with a piece of butter and some brown sugar, if you like.

4. Enclose each apple completely in the pastry, making sure that edges are well sealed. Refrigerate them for 30 minutes.

5. In a saucepan bring the water, sugar, and butter to a boil and boil gently for 5 minutes. Preheat oven to 425°.

6. Brush the apple dumplings with the sugar syrup and place them in the oven. Bake for 10 minutes and reduce the heat to 350°. Bake another 30 minutes, basting the dumplings every 10 minutes with the syrup. If you like, serve them with sweetened whipped cream.

Yield: 6 apple dumplings.

Notes and Variations

The apple cavities can be filled with anything you like. Try cinnamon, sugar, and butter, or even some apricot jam.

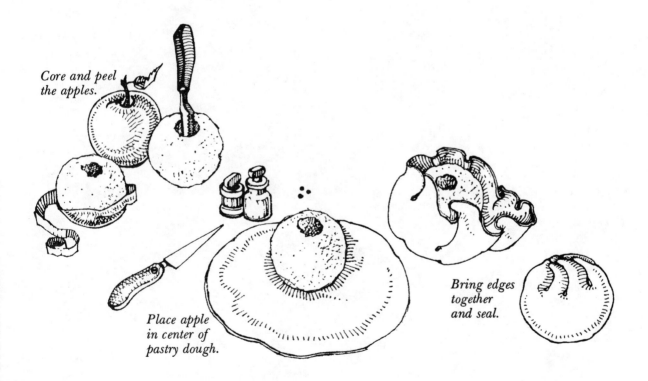

Core and peel the apples.

Place apple in center of pastry dough.

Bring edges together and seal.

The Sauces

Notes on Sauces

Where dumplings are prepared for use with soups, stews, or gravies, separate sauces are, of course, irrelevant. Other dumplings, however, are greatly enhanced by preparing an appropriate sauce or sauces to serve with them. For example, many of the Chinese dumplings cry for the presence of spicy soy-based dipping sauces, along with duck sauce and perhaps a mustard-vinegar sauce as well. While many of the Italian dumplings, such as gnocchi, ravioli, or capelletti, are happy with just butter and cheese, for variety you can also serve them with a tomato sauce or even a garlic pesto. Meat dumplings and quenelles insist on the gracing presence of a sauce, and even sweet dumplings will occasionally demand a sauce or syrup for company.

As is the case with all dumplings, I here urge you again to use these recipes only as a springboard for your imagination. Variety is the spice of food as well as life. Experiment and enjoy.

Vinegar-Soy Sauce I

½ cup soy sauce
2 scallions, finely chopped
1 clove garlic, finely chopped
   A few drops of hot oil (more if you like
      spicy sauce)
1 tablespoon white vinegar (rice vinegar if
      possible)
2 teaspoons sesame oil
½ teaspoon grated fresh ginger root
1 teaspoon sugar

Mix all ingredients together in a bowl and serve with any of the Chinese dumplings, Vietnamese shrimp fritters, oyster balls, or shrimp balls.

Vinegar-Soy Sauce II

½ cup soy sauce
3 tablespoons white vinegar (rice vinegar if
      possible)
2 teaspoons sesame paste or peanut butter
1 tablespoon fresh coriander, chopped
1 tablespoon dry sherry
½ teaspoon chili paste with garlic*
1 teaspoon oyster sauce*
3 scallions, finely chopped
1 clove garlic, finely chopped

Mix all ingredients together, and serve with any of the dumplings listed for Vinegar-Soy Sauce I.

*Available in oriental food stores.

Sweet And Sour Sauce

2 tablespoons tree ear mushrooms
2 cups water
⅔ cup red wine vinegar
1 cup sugar
1 teaspoon salt
1 tablespoon soy sauce
¼ cup peanut or vegetable oil
1 sweet red pepper or 1 sweet green pepper, seeded and coarsely chopped
1 large onion, cut into thin wedges
1 carrot, coarsely chopped
2 cloves garlic, peeled and crushed
1 tablespoon cornstarch, dissolved in 2 tablespoons water

1. Soak the mushrooms in very hot water for 30 minutes. Drain.*

2. Combine the water, vinegar, sugar, salt, and soy sauce in a saucepan and place over moderate heat. Stir until sugar dissolves. Simmer for 5 to 10 minutes.

3. Heat the peanut or vegetable oil in a skillet and add the mushrooms, all the other vegetables and the garlic. Stir-fry for 5 minutes.

4. Add the vegetables to the vinegar sauce, along with the dissolved cornstarch. Stir well and simmer for 10 minutes.

5. Remove from heat and serve with fried wonton.

Notes and Variations

*1. The tree ear mushrooms, which are sold in Oriental food stores, expand considerably when soaked, so make sure you use a large enough bowl.

2. The sauce can be made far ahead of time and reheated.

3. A few drops of red food coloring will turn the sauce the same color as that sauce served in Chinese restaurants.

Cho-Chang Sauce for Mandoo

⅓ cup soy sauce
2 tablespoons white vinegar (rice vinegar if possible)
½ teaspoon sugar
2 scallions, finely chopped
1 clove garlic, minced or put through a garlic press
2 tablespoons chopped peanuts (optional)

Mix all ingredients together in a small bowl and serve with mandoo.

Mustard-Vinegar Sauce

¼ cup powdered dry mustard
¼ cup cold water
2 tablespoons rice vinegar or use 1 tablespoon white vinegar plus 1 teaspoon water and ¼ teaspoon sugar
¼ teaspoon salt

1. Mix the mustard powder with a little of the cold water and blend to make a smooth paste.

2. Add the rest of the water and the vinegar gradually, stirring all the while. Add the salt.

3. Cover and refrigerate until ready to use. This sauce will keep for several weeks, covered, in the refrigerator.

Serve with any of the Chinese dumplings or pelmeni.

Duck Sauce

1 *cup mango chutney*
1 *cup apricot preserves*
¼ *cup cold water*

Place chutney, preserves, and water into the container of a blender (or food processor) and blend for just a few seconds to mix well and reduce to a fine consistency. Place in jar, cover, and refrigerate. Duck sauce will keep for a long time in the refrigerator.

Serve with any of the Chinese dumplings.

Tempura Sauce

1 *cup water*
½ *cup soy sauce*
1 *tablespoon sugar*
¼ *cup rice vinegar*
1 *teaspoon grated fresh ginger root*
1 *teaspoon grated Japanese radish (daikon)*
2 *tablespoons bonito flakes (optional)*
3 *scallions, finely chopped*

Combine all the ingredients in a bowl and refrigerate until ready to use. Serve with Tempura.

Mushroom Sauce for Fish and Shrimp Quenelles

This sauce goes well with almost any fish dish.

½ stick butter
¼ cup all-purpose flour
1½ cups hot fish stock or clam juice
½ cup dry white wine
¼ teaspoon thyme
¼ pound mushrooms, thinly sliced
3 tablespoons shallots, finely chopped
1 cup heavy cream
   Big pinch cayenne pepper
   Salt, if necessary
   Several grindings black pepper

1. Melt half the butter in a saucepan, and stir in the flour. Cook over low heat, stirring constantly, for 5 minutes.

2. Pour in the hot fish stock and wine, and beat with a whisk to eliminate any lumps. Add the thyme and cook over low heat for 20 minutes.

3. Melt the rest of the butter in a small skillet. Sauté the mushrooms and shallots for 5 minutes, then add to the fish stock. Cook over low heat, stirring frequently, for 30 minutes.

4. Add the cream and cayenne. Taste for seasonings and add salt and pepper as necessary. Heat, but do not boil, and serve.

Madeira Sauce

½ *stick butter*
4 *tablespoons flour*
2 *cups brown stock or canned bouillon*
  Salt and black pepper to taste
½ *cup Madeira*

1. Melt the butter in a saucepan and stir in the flour. Cook over low heat, stirring frequently for 10 minutes. Be careful not to burn this roux.

2. Bring the stock to a simmer and add to the roux. Beat with a wire whisk to blend well.

3. Cook over medium heat for about 15 minutes to reduce by about ½ cup. Season well with salt and pepper and add the Madeira. Simmer for a few minutes and serve.

Serve with chicken quenelles.

Avgolemono Sauce serve with Keftedes

3 *egg yolks*
1 *teaspoon cornstarch*
1 *cup hot chicken broth or water*
  Juice of 1 lemon
  Pinch of cayenne pepper
  Salt and pepper to taste
1 *tablespoon chopped fresh dill*

1. Combine the egg yolks and cornstarch in the top of a double boiler. Beat with a whisk until the mixture is light and frothy.

2. Add the hot broth or water, beating with a whisk all the time. Cook over simmering water until the sauce starts to thicken. Never let this sauce come anywhere near boiling—it will curdle.

3. Add the lemon juice and cayenne. Correct the seasoning.

4. Garnish with dill and serve.

Tomato Sauce I a hearty tomato sauce

4 *tablespoons olive oil*
2 *1-pound 12-ounce cans of imported Italian tomatoes, coarsely chopped*
1 *carrot, coarsely chopped*
1 *celery stalk, coarsely chopped*
1 *medium onion, coarsely chopped*
2 *tablespoons chopped fresh parsley*
4 *basil leaves, chopped* or *1 teaspoon dry basil*
½ *teaspoon sugar*
2 *teaspoons salt*
  Several grindings black pepper

1. Heat the olive oil in a large saucepan and add the vegetables and seasonings. Simmer for 1 hour.

2. Taste for salt and pepper and adjust if necessary.

3. Press the mixture through a sieve or a food mill. If consistency seems too watery, simmer over medium heat until the sauce thickens.

Serve with any of the Italian dumplings, or with eggplant or pepper fritters.

Tomato Sauce II a spicy tomato sauce

6 *tablespoons olive oil*
1 *medium onion, finely chopped*
1 *1-pound 12-ounce can imported Italian*
   tomatoes
2 *cloves garlic, finely chopped*
¼ *cup dry white wine*
2 *tablespoons chopped fresh parsley*
4 *basil leaves, chopped,* or 1 *teaspoon*
   dry basil
½ *teaspoon sugar*
1 *teaspoon salt*
   Several grindings black pepper
   Big pinch cayenne pepper
¼ *cup pitted black olives,*
   coarsely chopped

1. Heat the olive oil in a medium saucepan and add the onion. Sauté until onion is just soft.

2. Add the tomatoes, garlic, wine, herbs, and seasonings (not the olives) and simmer over low heat for 1 hour.

3. Add the olives and simmer for a few more minutes.

4. Check for seasoning and serve.

Serve with any of the Italian dumplings, or with eggplant or pepper fritters.

Tomato Sauce III a very delicate tomato sauce

1 stick butter
1 small onion, coarsely
   chopped
1 carrot, coarsely chopped
1 stick celery, coarsely chopped
2½ cups imported Italian canned tomatoes
2 teaspoons salt
¼ teaspoon sugar
½ cup heavy cream

1. Melt the butter in a medium saucepan. Add the onion, carrot, and celery, and sauté until they are just soft.

2. Add the tomatoes, salt, and sugar, and simmer for 1 hour.

3. Press the mixture through a sieve or food mill to make a puree and return to the saucepan. Add the cream and taste for seasoning. Heat through, but do not boil, and serve.

Serve with any of the Italian dumplings, or with eggplant or pepper fritters.

Lemon Sauce

½ cup sugar
1 tablespoon cornstarch
   Tiny pinch salt
1 cup water
2 tablespoons lemon juice
1 teaspoon grated lemon rind
2 tablespoons butter

1. Combine the sugar, cornstarch, salt, and water in a saucepan. Cook, stirring, until the mixture has thickened and is clear.

2. Remove from the heat and stir in the remaining ingredients.

Serve with lemon or pineapple fritters.

Pesto

2 cups fresh basil leaves
½ cup olive oil
2 tablespoons Pignoli (pine nuts)
2 garlic cloves
½ cup freshly grated Parmesan cheese
½ stick butter, softened to room temperature
Salt
Freshly ground black pepper

1. Use a blender or food processor to blend the basil, olive oil, pignoli, and garlic cloves.

2. Remove the mixture to a bowl and use a wooden spoon to beat in the cheese and the butter.

3. Taste for salt and adjust if necessary. Add a great deal of freshly ground pepper.

4. If the mixture seems too thick, beat in a tablespoon of hot water.

Serve with potato gnocchi.

Remoulade Sauce

1 cup mayonnaise
2 tablespoons Dijon mustard
1 tablespoon each finely chopped parsley, celery, and capers
¼ teaspoon tarragon
1 teaspoon chopped parsley
1 teaspoon anchovy paste

Combine all ingredients in a bowl. Chill in refrigerator until ready to use.

Serve with oyster or marinated shrimp fritters.

Anise Syrup

This syrup is poured over warm buñuelos just before serving.

3 *cups water*
1½ *cups brown sugar*
¼ *teaspoon anise seeds*

1. Place water, sugar, and anise seeds into a saucepan. Cook, stirring, over medium heat until the sugar has melted.

2. Bring to a boil and let boil for about 30 minutes or until the syrup has been reduced by a little more than half.

3. Remove from heat, but do not allow to become completely cold. Syrup should be warm, but not hot, when it is poured over the buñuelos.

4. To serve, pour about 2 tablespoons of syrup over each buñuelo.

Pineapple-Rum Sauce

1 *tablespoon cornstarch*
1 *cup pineapple juice*
⅓ *cup sugar*
  Pinch of salt
¼ *teaspoon grated lemon rind*
2 *tablespoons rum*
2 *tablespoons butter*

1. Combine the cornstarch with a little of the pineapple juice in a saucepan. When well blended, gradually stir in the remaining juice, sugar, and salt.

2. Cook, stirring, until the sauce thickens.

3. Remove from heat and stir in remaining ingredients.

Serve with pineapple fritters.

Raspberry Sauce

2 cups raspberries
½ cup sugar
1 tablespoon cornstarch
1 tablespoon lemon juice
1 tablespoon kirsch

1. Combine the raspberries with the sugar in a saucepan. Bring to a boil, stirring frequently. Taste for sweetness, and add more sugar if desired.

2. Remove from heat and strain.

3. Combine the cornstarch with a little of the raspberry mixture. Heat the remaining mixture and add the cornstarch mixture. Cook, stirring, until sauce has thickened.

4. Remove from heat and stir in lemon juice and kirsch.

Serve with lemon or Bulgarian yogurt fritters.

Index

C

D

E

F

J

K

L

M

N

O